Secrets of Success

Ayatullah Ja'far Subhani

Copyright

Copyright © 2021 al-Burāq Publications.

All rights reserved. No part of this publication may be reproduced, distributed, or transmitted in any form or by any means, including photocopying, recording, or other electronic or mechanical methods, without the prior written permission of the publisher, except in the case of brief quotations embodied in critical reviews and certain other noncommercial uses permitted by copyright law. For permission requests, write to the publisher, addressed "Attention: Permissions [Secrets of Success]," at the email address below.

ISBN: 978-1-956276-12-1.
Printed and published by al-Burāq Publications.

Ordering Information
We offer discounts and promotions for wholesale purchases and for non-profit organizations, libraries, and other educational institutions. Contact us at the email below for further information.

www.al-Buraq.org
publications@al-Buraq.org

First Edition | December 2021

Dedication

The publication of this book was made possible through the generous support of our donors.

Please recite *Sūrah al-Fātiha* and ask Allāh for the Divine reward (*thawāb*) to be conferred upon the donors and also the souls of all the deceased in whose memory their loved ones have contributed graciously towards the publication of *Secrets of Success*.

Duaa al-Hujja

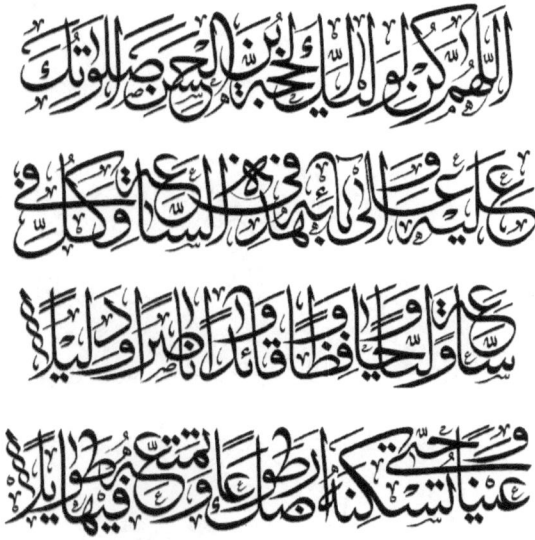

O Allah, be, for Your representative, the Hujjat (proof), son of al-Hasan, Your blessings be upon him and his forefathers, in this hour and in every hour: a guardian, a protector, a leader, a helper, a proof, and an eye - until You make him live on the Earth, in obedience (to You), and cause him to live in it for a long time.

Table of Contents

Introduction: The Period of Hopes and Aspirations..........1

Liking and Enthusiasm 5

    A Page from the Biography of a Famous Painter 6

    The Arrow Showing Aptitude 8

    Know Yourself 10

    Latent Capabilities 11

Unrelenting Effort 15

    Masterpieces Created in Prisons...19

    Work and Effort in the View of the Religious Leaders........20

Faith in Intention 25

    Huzaifah in the Court of Qaiser 27

Patience and Perseverance 33

    The Role of Steadfastness in Learning Art..........................37

    A Spring and a Mountain 38

Focus 43

    Aimless People 44

Discipline..49

Gradual Progress 55

    Why Should We Draw a Big Program?.................................55

    Why to Begin at a Low Level? 57

Avoid Blind Following 61

    A Unique Story...63

    The Tale of a Stupid Sufi 72

Counsel 77

History is the Best Teacher 83

    Making Use of Opportunities 87

    Youth is the Most Opportune Time 90

Firm Determination 95

    The Commander of the Faithful, Ali (a.s.) Orders His Son to Have Firm Determination 99

Awareness of Circumstances 105

    Institution of the Pope 108

    The Most Intelligent Man of the East 109

    Enemy: A Stepstone to Success 112

Failure is a Ladder to Success 115

    The Persian King Plucks Sweet Fruit from a Sour Tree ... 117

    The Defeat of Hitler 119

Courage and Fearlessness 123

    The Courage of Martin Luther in Bringing about Religious Reform 127

Self Sacrifice 131

Difficulties and Calamities 135

    Objection Raised by Materialists 140

Accepting the Reality 145

Flexibility 153

The Correct Way 159

Unexpected Success 163

    Luck, Stars and Predictions etc. 166

- Superstitious People of the West 169
- Blaming the Stars! 171

Waiting for a Chance 175

Incorrect Understanding of Destiny 181
- A Wrong Notion About Destiny 183
- Force of Environment 184
- Under the Shade of Allah's blessings 185

Inherited Wealth 189
- From a Tailoring Shop to the Presidential Chair 192

Introduction: The Period of Hopes and Aspirations

In the Name of Allāh, the Most Gracious, the Most Merciful

The period of youth is an age of aspirations and hopes. A time to be happy. This is the time when the future of every young person comes before his eyes in the form of sweet dreams. He begins to think. He makes programs and treasures grand ambitions in his heart.

However, sometimes it also happens that a man breaks down right during the time of his youth. Such a person is never able to achieve any of his aspirations, even till the time he becomes old.

Sometimes it also happens that, quite unexpectedly, a person obtains much beyond his expectations and all of his sweet dreams become reality.

Surely one man's success and another's failure are not accidental or without reason behind them. The causes of both must be sought in the very lives of the persons concerned.

We can be sure that one who succeeds has started life in a way, which assures his success and one who fails, most probably, does so due to his own mistakes. It is because he has walked a path that did not lead to his destination.

In this book, our aim is to describe the reasons for the success of the world's successful people so that the young generation may benefit by it and adopt the path, which is straight, and avoid the alleys, which are unknown and full of hurdles.

Secrets of success are not merely one or two. Though a part of their success is due to what they had obtained as legacy from their parents in the form of internal qualifications, natural traits and intelligence. Certainly such traits cannot be obtained by making efforts, as they are Divine gifts, which the Almighty

God has bestowed upon them for administering their worldly affairs.

This book will also prove that even though such factors facilitate the development of the youths they are not the sole determinants of a successful life.

Introduction: The Period of Hopes and Aspirations

The actual factors of progress are different and they are such that anyone who aspires to be successful can seek them out easily and use them to his advantage. By adopting such techniques he can certainly become a distinct member of the society if not one of the most successful persons of the world. Such an achievement too is praise-worthy and laudable, because, there are so many young people who miss the path of success and meet failure in life.

The progress of man mostly depends upon training, zest, struggle and proper programming. The readers will find these things in the following pages of the first part. The influence of 'heredity' is much less in comparison to them.

We shall now explain briefly the secrets of success illustrating the same by examples from the lives of great men.

Ja'far Subhani

Liking and Enthusiasm

One of the causes of success is taking up the vocation to your liking and that which commensurate to your intelligence or mental ability.

God has not created all of us alike. We all are not bestowed with the ability of doing everything. But, in order to run the society smoothly He has given a distinct taste and tendency to everyone. It is so, in order that one may take up the profession of ones own liking or bent of mind, and that, which attracts one; thus deriving benefit from ones natural competence.

Generally one of the causes of young people's failure and defeat is not following this established rule. As a result of wrong propaganda and faulty training they go after jobs, which are not according to their aptitude. They take up vocations for which they are not suitable.

They forget the accepted principle: "Every mind has certain predisposition. Lucky is the one who finds it out."

I remember that in the years 1951-53 the subject of oil had seized public attention. Every Iranian man and woman was thinking only about oil. The value of oil exports had soared high in the eyes of the Iranian society. This had caused a change in the thinking of the student community. All or most of the students desired to join the oil industry though many of them did not have a natural bent for it.

The progress and success of a student gets a lethal blow if he enters a field, which is not in line with his or her natural bent. For instance, if a youth is interested in literature, if his tongue and pen spread literary pearls and he has no liking at all for mathematics he will definitely not succeed except in the field of literature.

A Page from the Biography of a Famous Painter

Now let us read an extract from the diary of a famous painter: He was an idle boy during his college days. He neither studied properly nor allowed his companions to do so. He was a thorn both in his own path and that of others. Yet his appearance showed that he was a capable boy.

A professor who was an expert psychologist called him, gave him some advice and warned him of the bad consequences of his life-style. He counseled: Nobody is fortunate enough to have the protection of a father forever. Life is full of difficulties. The way you live will make you suffer badly in future...

However, the professor observed that when he was advising the boy he was busy drawing a picture with a piece of coal on the floor.

The intelligent professor at once understood that this boy was born to be an artist and had nothing to do with the problems of algebra. No amount of effort in the field of mathematics would benefit him.

Realizing his responsibility in this connection, he informed the boy's guardian of this discovery. He told the boy's father to the effect: "Your son is very much interested in drawing. If you change his faculty, he might earn much fame in art."

Days passed and the words of the professor came true. That boy soon became an expert painter.

Edison was asked by some, "Why most of the young people are unable to live a successful life?" He replied, "Because they are not aware of their path and they traverse other routes."

Such people prove harmful to the society in two ways: They do not adopt the vocation for which they are capable and wherein they can get success and another harm is that they take upon themselves a responsibility which they are unable to fulfill.

The Arrow Showing Aptitude

Every child is born with a sign, which shows the field of activity for which he is born. Lucky is the one whose guardians can read this sign in time. Nowadays the talents of the people are ascertained through vocational tests in advanced countries and they are advised to go for the course for which they are most suitable.

How nice it would have been if the scientist, along with instruments of measuring temperature and tremors, also invented something to measure the capacity and capability of people and install it in all educational institutions! It would have saved many people's talents.

Galileo was fond of making toys in his childhood. His parents ignored this aptitude of their son and got him admitted to a course in medicine. He could make no progress. Thereafter he studied Maths and Physics and as a result his talents in astronomy became apparent.

Galileo was the first one to prove that the earth revolves around the sun. He was the first to invent the pendulum, which was widely put to use in the manufacture of clocks.

Tolstoy loved books while yet a child. He read many books on philosophy. While reading he was trying to understand various issues about life. Till the end of his life he remained occupied in this field.

George Moreland took up drawing the figures of animals. His art became apparent from the time he was only six. Though he lived for only 41 years he left numerous memorable pieces of art.

The expertise of Zerah Calburn in mathematics could also be seen right from his childhood. Some times people used to ask him as to how many seconds were there in a year or more and he would give the correct answer in an instant.

James Watt was the inventor of many machines and the one who had discovered the power of steam. He was very fond of conducting experiments in his childhood. Subsequently he attained much fame in the world of physics.

Darwin had domesticated a number of animals in his childhood. This hobby encouraged him to study the lives of animals and the changes through which they passed. After making along journey he wrote a book classifying and describing the different kinds of animals and put forth a new theory of evolution.

Know Yourself

Our religious leaders have emphasized that we must know and be acquainted with ourselves; that we should delve deep to find out our inner self.

Our internal feelings are like a magnet attracting similar things. They store things or events in 'memory' so as to bring them out later when needed. Man is able to savor their benefits then.

If whatever we learn is in line with our inner aptitude then it is easily stored up in the treasury of our memory and remains safe for a long period.

But if we do a thing, which is contrary to our liking, then our mind forgets it soon. Thus the chances of our success are reduced.

One who has ignored his natural aptitude is like one who swims against the currents or like the one who has entrusted himself to the giant waves which could sweep him away to the other side. Such a man seldom succeeds in his work.

In short, when man becomes aware of his capabilities and knows his liking and then adopts a suitable vocation he soon becomes successful because he has a powerful inner attraction for the same.

Latent Capabilities

Some powers appear at a certain time. An able and expert psychologist can detect them. Sometimes it so happens that a person appears a slow learner in the early stage of his schooling. But the same student proves to be intelligent later on. Obviously, particular conditions are required for the blossoming of such talents.

It is said that Einstein, who was a great scholar and mathematician of his time used to fail in his primary school examinations. But in particular circumstances his competence came out shining.

Sometimes it so happens that an officer appears to be mild and timid for sometime. But when the occasion arises he exhibits such bravery and courage that onlookers become spellbound.

News reached Malik Shah, the Seljuk king that the Qaiser of Rome was planning to conquer Baghdad. The Shah moved toward the borders of Iran with his regular army.

His Minister Khwaja Nizamul Mulk was once inspecting the forces when he spotted a short-stature soldier. He ordered that he should be brought out of the ranks.

He was of the opinion that a man of such a short stature would not be of any use in the army. But Malik Shah told his vizier, "How do you know? Maybe this man captures the Qaiser himself."

Finally the Muslims were victorious and this soldier was the one to capture the Qaiser!

Unrelenting Effort

The system of world and every page of human history testify that everybody's success is invariably related to his efforts. It takes hundreds of chemical actions and reactions for a small plant to become a big tree. Every living thing naturally knows that its existence depends upon struggle and efforts.

There are several reasons why our youths fail in their professions. One of the reasons of such failure is lack of continuous effort.

The rush of promising youths toward minor organizations shows that they have lost the enthusiasm and longing for great jobs. Consequently they become consumers of wealth instead of producers.

Lives of successful men show that each of them were ever struggling hard workers always making relentless efforts t0wards their goals.

Alexander Hamilton, a thinker and an intelligent man of his time says, "People say that I am very intelligent. But I am unaware of any such thing. I only know that I am merely a hardworking person."

Another wise man says, "Whatever I am today is merely the result of my effort. I have not partaken even a single morsel that was not earned by me with my own effort." All the wonderful inventions are the fruits of untiring efforts of the scientists. The inventor of radio sometimes worked through the night while his family members slept soundly.

Edison, in order to complete some of his inventions, did not come out of his laboratory for days together. With an aim to control electrical energy in a way that its use may be cheap and easy, he often remained inside his laboratory for two or three days at a stretch. Sometimes he even forgot to eat. At other times he took only a few bites of dry bread and returned to his work immediately.

In the life history of the great French scholar, Pasteur, we see that the basic principle of his life was 'work'. Sometimes he was so deeply engrossed in his work that he could not hear anything outside. So much so that when the Germans surrounded Paris and the guns were roaring, making deafening noise Pasteur was busy in his laboratory.

Napoleon slept only five hours a day and was busy the remaining nineteen hours daily.

A very intelligent scientist of the East, Ibne Sina (Avicenna) was a very studious and hardworking person. His numerous books on various subjects are the fruits of his relentless efforts. His masterpiece in philosophy *Shifa* and another of his great work *Canon* in medicine have earned global fame. Another of his book has been translated into several languages of the world.

Not a single day of the great Muslim scholar Ibne Rushd passed without reading and contemplating ever since he learnt how to read.

Jawahiral Kalam is a very valuable book and the fountainhead of Islamic jurisprudence. Till date no other Fiqh book has been written so comprehensively. Its last edition consists of around forty bulky volumes.

Muhammad Taqi Qummi is a great Iranian personality living in Egypt. He says, "When I showed all the aforesaid volumes to the professors in the University of Egypt and told them that all these books have been written so minutely by a single person they were astounded."

Another great scholar, the late Shahabadi, who was an expert in science, philosophy and scholastic theology, narrates that his father was one of the students of the writer of *Jawahir- al Kalam*. One day when that great scholar's great and intelligent son passed away and it was nearly midnight by the time bathing and covering of the body was over, it was decided to put the corpse in one of the rooms around the shrine of Imam Ali (a.s.) till the next morning so that more people may be able to attend the burial.

Though the author of *Jawaahir* had suffered a shocking blow just a few hours ago he did not postpone his routine reading and writing after reciting some parts from the holy Quran besides the body of the departed son. Thus he gave a proof of his extraordinary patience, endurance and fortitude.

The great Islamic jurisprudent, Agha Burujardi says: One night I was pondering over a problem of the principles of jurisprudence and making notes. I was so much engrossed in this that I forgot that it was time to go to bed. When I heard the Morning Azan I realized that it was dawn and that I had been working the whole night.

Let us now consider this. All of us have heard folk tales regarding treasures that lie buried in the earth guarded by huge dragons and that unless we overcome the dragon we cannot get the treasure. Though some believe it to be true the majority thinks it is just folklore. But let us think this way: Those treasures are, in fact, the mental or physical capabilities, which have been bestowed upon man, and the dragons are the barriers and difficulties, which come in the way of attaining those treasures.

Edison says, "None of my discoveries was accidental. Whenever it came to my mind that a certain work would be beneficial I used to engage myself in it. Then I used to conduct experiment after experiment until I succeeded."

Newton has said, "If I have reached any elevated status, it is only the result of work and effort."

Mc Launge says, "If people knew how much troubles I have taken upon myself for attaining this position of a tutor they would not feel surprised at my wonderful success."

In the words of Buzurgmehr, "Mouth must be kept shut and hands free; we must go on working with our hands and never talk of rest and should have faith that the golden key to success is effort."

Masterpieces Created in Prisons

Really, some people are indeed great. They remain restless like the waves of the sea. Love for work and longing for the goal keeps them busy forever and to such an extent that they do not cease working even in the most difficult moments of their lives.

The great Muslim historian, Ibne Khaldun, had written his masterpiece *Muqaddimah* during his exile.

The famous philosopher of the East, Khwaja Nasiruddin Tusi was imprisoned by the Ismailis at 'The Fort of Death'. He wrote his world famous book *Ishaaraat* there.

Our great scholar, Shahid-e-Awwal had authored his precious book on the Islamic Laws, *Lumaa* in the prison of Damascus.

The History of the World was written by Sir Walter in jail.

Robin Crumm had authored many famous literary books during detention...

We conclude this discussion here and present the words of wisdom uttered by our respected religious leaders about hard work.

Work and Effort in the View of the Religious Leaders

The Holy Prophet (s.a.w.a.) once saw a laborer whose hand had swollen up. The Holy Prophet raised his hand up and exclaimed, "The fire of Hell will never burn this hand. This hand is loved by Allah and His Prophet. Whosoever lives on his hand's earnings will receive Allah's blessings and mercy."

Unrelenting Effort

A worshipper once came into the presence of the Prophet and the Prophet was told that this person passes the whole year in worship and the maintenance of his family members is borne by his brother. The Holy Prophet said, "His brother, who bears the expenditure of this man's family is nearer to Allah than this man. That man's worship is more precious than of this."

Once Amirul Mo-mineen Ali (a.s.) saw a group of people sitting in the mosque of Kufa. On inquiry he was informed that they were 'Rijalul Haqq' meaning, they eat if someone gives them to eat otherwise they endured with patience.

Amirul Mo-mineen averred, "The dogs in the streets of Kufa are also doing like that." Then he ordered that the 'Rijalul Haqq' should be dispersed and that everyone must work to earn his livelihood.

Good fortune and prosperity comes to those who make efforts and work for it, not to the idle ones.

Those who have shaken the world were not extraordinary from the viewpoint of brainpower. The cause of their victory was hard work, effort and perseverance.

The great personalities of the world never hesitated to do small jobs for making both ends meet. Many of the brilliant students of Imam Ja'far Sadiq (a.s.) were oil vendors, cobblers and camelhirers.

Plato used to make up the expenses of his journeys by selling oil. The Famous botanist, Lena was a shoemaker.

It is pitiable that people look down at the job of coolies, though carrying weight is a gentleman's honest work. If the Dockers at port or laborers of a city stop working even for a day everything would come to a stand still.

The great leader of mankind, Amirul Mo-mineen Hazrat Ali (a.s.) planted orchards with his own hands and later donated them to the needy people.

He had installed many tents in various parts of Medina with his strong hands. He was never ashamed of doing hard work.

The Prophet of Islam (s.a.w.a.) had condemned a person who became a burden for society and said that such a person remains away from Allah's mercy.

Our fifth Imam, Imam Muhammad Baqir (a.s.) used to work in his fields and orchards even during the hot season and perspire there. He worked hard and also exhorted his men to do likewise.

Once his friend, Muhammad Mankadar took exception to this. He was of the opinion that it was not befitting for a personality of the Imam's stature to toil like this. Imam told him, "To earn by ones own work is a kind of worship. Through this I want to make myself and my family needless of you and others."

Faith in Intention

Faith or belief in ones aim is such an inner motive force, which definitely takes one to the final goal. Man loves himself too much and this love never abates. From this view if one is convinced that ones welfare and success lies in a particular work he would definitely proceed towards it.

One who values ones health takes the most bitter medicine in case of illness and finds that it easy to do so. He even puts himself on the operation table if necessary. Why? Because he knows that his safety is in taking that bitter medicine and his welfare demands the cutting off of certain diseased parts of his body.

If the diver is sure that there are precious pearls at the bottom of the ocean he submits himself to the waves of the sea with a particular zeal and enthusiasm. But if his belief were weak he would remain sitting idle on the shore and never venture into the deep waters.

Man steels his will power to attain some goal under the influence of such belief and faith that he does not care for the difficulties, hurdles and bitterness on the road to his goal. He befriends the thorns in his path and never complains of pain.

Sometimes the love for attaining a goal is so strong that man does not care even for his life. He sacrifices himself for his aim. He even greets death with a smiling face and sacrifices his life for his goal. Someone has correctly said:

Shall I tell you the sign of a Faithful Man?

If death approaches him he embraces it with a smiling face.

It is the same trust and faith in the aim that carries the astronauts high up into the thresholds of death. They risk their lives to discover the mysteries of space and exploit them for the benefit of mankind. They struggle hard relentlessly and courageously to attain this goal.

Fourteen hundreds years ago the Muslims were not more than 313 in number and they did not have enough weapons when they faced the powerful army of Quresh at Badr. From the viewpoint of warfare experts there was remote chance of the Muslim victory. It was unimaginable that such a little group of Muslims would scatter the powerful army of Quresh. But contrary to the thinking of Materialist the small group, which was armed with Faith, overpowered the physically strong opponents within hours. The cause of the victory of the tiny minority was the same Faith, which had made it very easy for them to sacrifice their lives in the path to their goal. This truth was also accepted by their enemies. Before the Badr encounter, a brave soldier of the unbelievers was asked to ascertain the material and spiritual power of the Muslims. He said, "Though the Muslims are much less than us in number and also inferior in material power they are much more strong in spirituality and steadfastness in the path of their religion. They are a group whose shield is their sword. None of them would die unless and until he kills at least one of your warriors. What can we gain when they kill an equal number of our men?"

Huzaifah in the Court of Qaiser

A warrior who has complete faith in his goal never hesitates in sacrificing anything. For him there remains no difference between the nuptial bed and the battlefield.

The history of Islam is replete with such examples and we come across such incidents in the history of others communities also. A brigadier was arrested along with his men by the Byzantine army. The martial court of the enemy sentenced all the Muslim prisoners to death and ordered their massacre. The said brigadier was told that if he becomes a Christian the court would reverse its decision.

But the Muslim commander valued his aim more than his life. He knew that even if he gives up Islam apparently and becomes a Christians just for show, the resolve of all the other Muslim warriors who had fought courageously would also weaken and they would be deceived by the conspiracy of the enemy.

Thinking on these lines he rejected the court offer in unequivocal terms. Then the court promised that if he (Huzaifah) embraces Christianity the daughter of Qaiser would be given to him in marriage, and moreover he would be given a high position, but he rejected this offer too.

Emperor Qaiser was personally present in the court. He ordered that one of the commander's men be thrown in boiling oil so that he may see with his own eyes that the court's decision was serious and not a joke.

Huzaifah witnessed his man being thrown into the boiling oil and saw his flesh coming away from his bones and being dispersed in boiling oil. Seeing this Huzaifah wept in grief.

The enemy thought that Huzaifah was weeping due to fear. But suddenly he turned toward the courtiers and spoke thus: "I am not weeping over the consequences of this man. I myself am awaiting for

Faith in Intention

this end. I grieve because I have only one life to sacrifice on Islam. If only I had as many lives as the number of my hair, I would have sacrificed all of them on my religion." Those who heard these words were extremely astonished at this unflinching faith and under some pretext they released Huzaifah along with his eighty companions.

In the world of politics today there is a problem called 'Vietnam'. It was a poor nation having the power of bow and arrow only but it has complete faith and trust in its aim. This nation brought down America's vast economy and administration on its knees. In fact only one 'Viet Kong' compelled America to spend 10,00,000 dollars.

In the year 1965 alone America dropped 80,000 bombs on South Vietnam (which is under the control of Viet Kong) and on North Vietnam and in 1966 America had to spend 15,80,00,00,00 dollars in these hostilities.

We see today the religious leaders of the Buddhists immolate themselves in the fields of 'Saigon' without the least sign of grief on their faces as they burn like a candle before the eyes of their followers who surround them singing religious songs. All this is only due to their unflinching faith and therefore their land has today become the battlefields for the east and west.

On the other hand, for creating courage and determination America has to dispatch a group of artists at a huge cost to provide light to the darkened hearts of their soldiers by dance and other material entertainment.

The Vietnamese soldiers are fighting for a particular aim and their goal is to end the rule of injustice and oppression and live freely, while the American soldier does not know what he is fighting for because there is a distance of thousands of miles between his country and Vietnam.

There are many examples of faith in aim. The greatest sign of Faith is that one bets ones life on it. The Holy Quran has mentioned this very clearly.

Patience and Perseverance

Patience and perseverance, tolerance and forbearance are common traits of the world's most successful people. Patience is a very high quality of man.

Sometimes one errs in differentiating between patience on one hand and laziness, inaction, tolerating oppression and relying on luck on the other. Whereas patience and forbearance guarantees victory and success while laziness and inaction causes misfortune and results in failure.

Now we shall explain the difference between these two opposing qualities illustrating them through different examples:

A gardener desires that there be so many flowers in his garden that it always remains fragrant and the different colors of the flowers please the eyes and the atmosphere of the garden remains good.

If the gardener wants it to be so he must work hard. He should endure the sun and heat and cold and rain. He must become habituated to the pricking of thorns also and he ought to visit his garden often.

Hardships that one must endure to attain the goal are termed as patience.

If a trader wishes to earn profits and increase his wealth he must undertake arduous land, sea and air journeys. If a student desires good marks, a diplomat intends to woo the people they must work hard with utmost steadfastness and determination.

Regarding this Hafiz Shirazi says:

Patience and success are friends of each other, Success comes as a result of patience.

One may wonder why as the causes of success 'steadfastness and firm resolve' is not discussed along with 'work and effort'. It is so because there is a difference between the two. There are some people who do make efforts in the beginning, yet they break down when confronted with difficulties. Looking from this angle, steadfastness and endurance should be regarded as the supports of work and effort. They must be considered as the motive forces assuring that the work continue unceasingly.

Every triumph is not of the same kind. Sometimes it arrives early and sometimes it takes a long time. One must not expect that everything would be done in the same manner and that everything will end in success.

Patience and Perseverance

Works differ from one another. There are some easy jobs, which must be undertaken in difficult circumstances. Moreover the capacities and capabilities of people also are different. It is possible but the degrees of their intelligence may not be the same.

If a man is able to learn a vocation and becomes habituated to endure difficulties of the field within a year it does not necessarily mean that another person would also require the same time to master the same line of work.

It is said that George Stephenson, the mathematician who also came to be known as the father of the steam engine was very slow in learning and in making educational progress. Yet he manufactured the world's first railway engine. He produced the world's first passenger train in 1825.

Scholars say: High intelligence is of two types: one is late-coming intellect and another, which come soon.

The lives of great men show this disparity. Hence we can say that success is also of two types: one comes sooner and the other, late.

So if success does not arrive early one must not give up efforts. One must not imagine that victory is impossible and very difficult. A great Muslim scholar Abu Ja'rana is famous for his firm determination and steadfastness. He has said, "I have learnt firm determination from an insect called 'Bijju'. Once I was sitting near a clean and shining pillar in the Jame Masjid when I observed that the tiny insect was attempting to climb the upright stone pillar to reach a lamp that was on the top. I kept sitting whole night and observing until dawn that how relentlessly that insect was struggling to climb up the slippery column. I counted 700 attempts when he was falling down from the middle of the path because the pillar was very smooth and glassy. His legs could not hold on. I was extremely astonished to see the extraordinary determination of that little worm. As it was time for Morning Prayer I got up from my place, made ablution and engaged myself in worship. After concluding my Namaz I looked back toward the pillar to find to my absolute astonishment that, as a result of its perseverance and untiring effort the insect had achieved its aim and was sitting close to the burning light!"

In the words of a melodious poet: Firm determination and perseverance is a nail. Man must take a lesson from it. The more you hit on it, the more firmly it sticks into its place.

The Role of Steadfastness in Learning Art

'Demotson' is a great American orator who had to face failure a number of times while learning the art of public speaking and consequently had to stop speaking for some time. But he was not one who would give up so easily and in order to perfect his art he began to practice in his cellar. Sometimes he shaved half his face to look satirical so that he may be compelled to remain indoors and continue his practice. At last he succeeded.

The story of a famous seventh century Muslim scholar, 'Sakkaki', is also very interesting. He began to study at the age of thirty. Though his teachers were not at all hopeful of his success he continued his study with a wonderful zeal and enthusiasm. With a view to ascertain the extent of his intelligence a teacher once posed a problem of Shafei jurisprudence before him. The teacher said, "The Shaykh says that the skin of a dog becomes clean and pure by pounding." Sakkaki was supposed to learn this by heart. So he repeated it many times and became ready to recite it when called for. Next day the teacher asked him to recite the sentence in front of all the other students. He stood up at once to say, "The dog said, the teacher's skin becomes clean and pure by pounding." Hearing this, everyone, including the teacher burst into laughter. Yet the aged pupil's determination was so sound that despite this experience he did not give up his study, but followed the same course for another ten years. Of course, due to advancing age, his grasping power was becoming weak day by day. Once he had gone to the forest to memorize his lessons where he noticed that drops of rainwater constantly fell on a rock and made marks on that hard stone. He thought over it and told himself, "My heart is not harder than this rock. If drops of knowledge fall on it constantly like these raindrops they too would certainly leave imprints on it, at least to some extent." He returned home and began to study with added zeal. At last, as a result of his untiring and continuous efforts and nonstop endeavor he became a distinguished personality of the literary circles of the Arab world. He authored a book, which was, for many years, a textbook in the course of Arabic education.

A Spring and a Mountain

A spring or a rivulet always flows from the mountain downwards. On its path it has to face many obstructions. Sometimes its water does not move further for several hours. Hurdles try hard to restrict its flow but it does not relent in its effort to push forward and weaken the hurdles every moment. Finally it succeeds in carving out its course by any means and in any way.

Patience and Perseverance

Another example is worth attention. The late Malik-us-Shor-aa "Bahaar" has put this truth in verse thus:

A rivulet sprang from a mountain. A rock came in its way.

It asked mildly to the rock: O kind one, please give me way.

But since the rock had a rigid heart, it slapped it and told it harshly to go away from there.

I am not to move from here even if there is a flood.

Who are you to make me move? Why should I care for you? The spring did not get disappointed with this harsh lofty claim. It kept on putting pressure and tried hard to find a way.

By making constant effort you can attain anything you like.

Those who engage in public welfare require more patience, perseverance, endurance and steadfastness. Unless they have these virtues they cannot move a step further.

An English philosopher was of the view that anybody can do anything. In the light of this principle he went out riding with a companion. On their way they came across a low wall. The expert rider spurred his horse and crossed it. The philosopher attempted to do so but could not succeed and he fell off his mount. But he got up and tried again, but again he failed. Then at last he succeeded in crossing the wall.

'Odobon' was a famous American zoologist who had drawn some pictures and after that he went on a journey putting away the papers safely in a box. But during his absence a rat chewed away those pictures and on returning home when he opened the box he saw that all his hard work was destroyed and he became very sad. Yet he remained determined and drew all the pictures afresh.

Carlyle had written a volume on the history of France. A friend of his borrowed the first volume though it was the only copy with him. This book was destroyed in fire due to the carelessness of the friend's servant. With profound patience and perseverance Carlyle rewrote that volume.

Harvey had discovered blood circulation but he continued experimenting for eight years. Only then did he become sure of this. Then he put forth his view with simple arguments but met with strong opposition from all sides. A group called him mad and a lunatic. His friends began to avoid his company but he continued to defend his stand strongly. Today his view is accepted by all and is considered a fact of science.

Focus

One of the causes of success is focus or total attentiveness. As a consequence of centering thoughts on a single point the mind remains attached to it. Then even the hardest hurdle cannot weaken the man's concentration.

Focus is for work what a lever is for lifting weights.

The principle of a lever is that force concentrates at one point, which makes it easy to lift up heavy objects. Similarly by concentrating the mental powers on a single point one is able to solve complex problems.

The working of our mind and body is like that of raindrops.

When collected at one place they make a vast ocean. But if they fall here and there in scattered manner they disappear in the dust with out any visible effect.

We all must have heard about the great personality of Shaikh Bahai. He had mastery over many sciences like physics, mathematics and Islamics and has left a number of his precious books for the posterity. He says, "I have debated with many scientists and scholars. Though their knowledge was very wide in every field I used to win the debate. However when I came across a person who was a specialist in his field, he vanquished me easily. It was so because my knowledge was insufficient in that particular subject.

Mental abilities resemble the sunrays in the matter of solving problems. If sunrays are made to concentrate on a certain point with the help of a magnifying glass they burn down whatever is kept there. Though the scattered rays do not affect anything.

In the same way unless the rays of human thoughts focus on a point they cannot remove hurdles, as the different aspects are not illuminated. Veteran teachers always instruct their students to study everything deeply which only means that the thoughts must concentrate on a particular subject. All inventions and discoveries are the result of concentrated effort.

Aimless People

There are some of us who do not have any particular aim in life. They wander here and there like a drifting ship that dashes against submerged rocks. We can also compare it to an aeroplane without a compass. People without a program of action also smash against the rocks of difficulties or sink in an ocean of nothingness.

There also are some people who do have some program of activities but midway to their goal backtrack and begin to walk in another direction. Only those succeed who do not leave their path before reaching their goal and even if the journey is very long it does come to an end after continuous travel.

Some people fail despite being active and prepared because their mind is not constant. It wavers and jumps from one place to another. They step in different fields, starting a new venture before completing the previous one. They are jack-of-all-trades but master of none and they are not perfect in any particular field.

Nature has taught us a nice lesson. If we continue to uproot a sapling and put it in another place over and over again it would wither away and cannot grow up. But a plant that remains firmly rooted at the same spot grows into a huge tree. Then it flowers and also bears fruit.

Want of concentration or hesitation is same as a plant that is uprooted every now and then. So it neither flowers nor gives fruits. Rather it withers away and dies.

It is rightly said that concentrating the thoughts at one point is the hallmark of the wise.

Taking up many assignments together brings personal loss and also harms the society. It can damage a nation's economy and culture and result in anarchy, which is difficult to control.

Boron used to say: Man's interest and natural talent implies that he can concentrate his conscience and feelings on one point.

Newton was asked how he was able to discover so many things. His answer was that by constantly thinking about them. He was thinking on a subject so thoroughly and deeply that the subject became as clear as daylight before him.

A special feature of the modern civilization is specialization. We have experts in all walks of life. Specialization has become so necessary that the world cannot advance in its absence.

Discipline

Not only that discipline is a secret of the success of great men, our universe also stands on the same foundation. If the solar system is working regularly, if the stars are revolving around the sun systematically and if there is no flaw in this function for millenniums it is only due to the fact that the solar system is based on order.

Order is found in everything around us from the largest bodies of the universe to the minutest thing called 'atom'. Everything in this world is made up of tiny atoms. A wonderful discipline is in action and it is seen in each and every movement of the universe. There are tiny atoms in every system.

Every atom has its own center, which is called 'proton'. Many 'electrons' move round the center like stars and moons. In the words of a great Muslim scholar: "If you tear up the heart of every atom you will find its sun in its center."

The universe is the best guide for all of us. We should learn about life and the causes and reasons of its stability and success from it. This universe tells that: "The secret of my survival is the regularity and orderliness which my Creator has ingrained in me."

If the educational system of any country becomes chaotic, if the trade and economy of any nation is disturbed, if the balance of supply and demand is upset, if the law and order of any country turns corrupt, if the army gets out of control the end of that nation becomes certain.

When the commander of the Faithful, Ali (a.s.) was fatally injured by the sword of Ibne Muljim, the first bequest uttered by him to his sons, after advising them to refrain from Allah's disobedience, was regarding this orderliness in every affair: "I advise you to refrain from disobeying Allah and to abide by law and order and regularity in life."

One of the ways of orderliness is to divide our daily time according to our needs. Doing every necessary work in its proper time is life. We should further this foundation of life. We must refrain from disorderliness and indiscipline because irregularity ends propriety and destroys our talent and competence.

The leader of the God-fearing people Ali (a.s.) says, "A Muslim must divide his time into three parts. One part should be reserved for Allah's worship, one for earning livelihood and the third for attending to the demands of the body which cannot be ignored."

Discipline

If there was no orderliness or discipline in our past life can we benefit from such orderliness in the remaining years of our life?

"Certainly, we can..." because the three stages of our life, viz, childhood, youth and old age are like three compartments of a ship which can be separated from one another by pressing a button. If a compartment is damaged it can be separated from the rest.

Only he is successful who can, using his wisdom, separate different compartments of his life and deal with them separately.

It is pitiable that man, instead of gaining from the present opportunities, should remain sorrowful for his past, thus wasting the time available to him and become careless about bringing order in the forthcoming time.

A competent minister was carrying out his administrative duties with the help of his assistants. When asked as to how he was arranging his affairs he replied, "I never postpone today's work for tomorrow. In my view it is not correct to delay anything."

We see signs in offices and workshops saying: Time is Gold. It surprises me because the value of time becomes more than gold if everything is done in time.

Gradual Progress

We should start working on a small scale. But this does not mean that we should begin with little courage.

What we mean is that we may prepare an elaborate and lengthy program and also start working on it with great courage but we should not try to hurry through all the things simultaneously. Rather we should advance little by little and achieve our goal gradually.

Why Should We Draw a Big Program?

Because those who have lofty thoughts and high intelligence cannot limit their courage in small circles. They intend to pursue a new aim as soon as they achieve the first one. Therefore it is necessary to make a big program right from the beginning. Human psychology also demands it. Unless a man does not ready himself for a big goal he cannot attain his aim and sometimes he is unable to obtain even half of it.

Narrow-minded and coward people remain content with their present condition and want to remain where they are, but people having high ideals and foresight begin their job with lofty thoughts and always try to improve their condition.

Saduddin Taftazani was one of those great Islamic scholars who founded the art of eloquence in Islam. Once intending to gauge the courage of his son he asked him, "What is your aim in acquiring knowledge?"

"I want to acquire as much knowledge as you have."

He was sorry to see this low aim of his son and told him regretfully, "If your courage is only this much then you will not reach even half of it. Your thinking is very narrow. I am your father Saduddeen. I had heard about the marvelous knowledge of Imam Ja'far Sadiq (a.s.) and was appreciating his high position through his memorable narrations of Hadith. From the beginning of my primary stage it was my endeavor to reach the standard of knowledge of this great man. Despite such a high ideal. I could attain only the position, which you are now observing, while this is nothing compared to the knowledge of the great leader. Therefore, if your aim is so low, you will attain very little knowledge and one day you will give up the pursuit." Hence it is necessary for us to begin with great courage. A Persian couplet of admonition says:

Always cultivate great courage because the great men of the world have reached some status only due to great courage.

Rumi says: If there is continuous hunger and hirst and the water in the stomach is continuously boiling therein up and down.

Why to Begin at a Low Level?

The initial stage of any job is an experimental one wherein the exact idea about its benefits and harms is not quite clear. Maybe there are some obstacles in the path of the aim, which may require a long time for their removal.

It is also possible that we have adopted a path, which may not be leading to the goal we have in mind. Perhaps we have made some mistakes in drawing the program. Therefore, if we begin our work on a high level it might become difficult to correct our mistakes to remedy the situation by changing the strategy.

We oriental people have this defect that we begin our jobs on a high level with much pomp. In such a condition it is quite difficult to change the path leaving the wrong road. As a result we may lose both, precious years of our life as well as our money, become disappointed and courageless and remain where we are.

We read in the diary of Nasiruddin Shah that he had gone on a tour of Europe. In London he met the

British Queen. He wanted to know the reason of a British bank's successful functioning in Iran. Hence he asked the Queen, "When this bank had opened its branch in the capital of Iran it began to function with a very little investment. How did it achieve so much progress so soon?"

The Queen replied to the effect, "Britishers do not reveal the secrets of their success to others. But due to our respect for you I shall mention one point. We, the westerners, especially the British, begin our work always on a low scale, so that in case we do not succeed, we may have an avenue for return and we may be able to change our strategy with a little loss. And if we achieve some benefit we expand our field at once. In this respect we are totally different from eastern people."

We ourselves have seen people who invested money without keeping the aforesaid point in mind and, consequently suffered much loss. They were then engulfed in difficulties and economic crisis.

Now we may look at the success of the Holy Prophet (s.a.w.a.). Millions of Muslims are proud to follow him. At the beginning of the call of Islam their number could be counted on ones fingers.

The Holy Prophet's program was so vast that it covered all the field of human life, be it politics or economics, morals or anything else. Moreover his program was perfect in every respect.

In the beginning the Holy Prophet did not demand from the people except the acceptance of belief in the 'Two witnesses' that is, belief in Only One God and in his being the prophet or messenger of Allah.

The Holy Prophet's great work had started on a little measure. He created the atmosphere little by little and issued commandments one by one for each and every aspect of human life and guided the entire humanity with such a great program that it changed the course of their life tremendously.

Avoid Blind Following

One of the secrets of success is to refrain from following others blindly. It is because such thoughtless following amounts to a war against our human nature.

We should not start copying those deeds of others for which we are not competent. We must also understand that the tendency of copying others in every way leads to failure.

As a rule, if the personality of some people remains defective and if they sometimes face failure and deprivation, it is so because they start moving without keeping in mind the extent of their ability. They ought to have made up their shortcomings by following some other path.

Becoming proud, envying others, remaining unaware of facts and situations are the defects, which make men copy others blindly even though, right from the beginning, they know nothing about what is to come at a later stage.

The Master of the Pious, Imam Ali (a.s.) has divided people into three categories: "People are either scholars or students. The third group is comprised of those who are ever ready to respond to every call. They are like mosquitoes being swept away with the wind. They fly in the direction of the wind without anything like self-will."

Such type of people, instead of trying to making their capabilities blossom put a lid on their intelligence and waste it away. These people always look around for the wings of others to fly with. They are ignorant of the fact that in this world of creation no two individuals are born with exactly equal capabilities in every field. No one can be equal to any other person in every respect, be it a matter of appearance, feeling or likes and dislikes. The lines on the palms of one man are always different from those of all others.

When the situation is such it is very unwise on our part to bind our thinking with the thoughts of others and not to take benefit of the individual God-given abilities, faculties and proficiencies.

Great people always tread their own new path. They have walked on ways, which others did not tread before. They have gifted new presents to humanity. Such great people have, throughout their lives, been innovators, giving birth to new ideas, sciences and industries.

The secret of Descartes' success in the field of science was that one day he purged his mind of all

Avoid Blind Following

his earlier knowledge in every science, especially in philosophy, and also gave up all of his earlier thoughts and theories. In this manner he turned all certainties too into doubts. He doubted everything so much that he doubted whether he himself existed?

On this basis he succeeded in bringing about a change in all the branches of philosophy. Had he too followed, like others, scholastic philosophy he would not have attained this success.

Great men always think independently. They believe that freedom from the bondage of the thoughts of others is the golden key to success. In their opinion, be it a personal matter or a social affair, blind following is suicidal.

A Unique Story

In the past, public baths used to have bugles and horns. In order to announce that the hot water bath had opened the owners blew the bugles an hour before dawn.

One day the bugle of a bath went missing or was out of order. To meet this emergency, the owner purchased a new bugle at a very high price and did his job. He paid ten times the cost to meet the situation.

The same day a foreigner arrived in the city. When he saw that there a thing costing one rial could be sold for ten rials he became very happy. He decided to purchase many bugles for sale there at a handsome profit. He did so accordingly and spread his merchandise in the big city square. He had thought that people would rush to buy his bugles but no one came to him despite a very long wait.

By chance, an old wealthy businessman with a walking stick in hand passed by him and asked him the reason of bringing in so many bugles and horns there. The poor man told him about his idea. The wise trader was astonished to see the folly of that person and said, "But did not you see that there are only two baths in this city? What was the use of importing so many bugles? Anyway, in order to help you, tomorrow I will perform a trick so that all your bugles sell out within a week."

"What will you do?" the man asked.

The trader told him, "You have nothing to do with it. Just know that the people of this city are great imitators and they seldom think over anything. I will take benefit of their weakness in your favor."

He borrowed a bugle from the seller and asked his servant to keep it in his house. Early next morning

Avoid Blind Following

that old trader went around the town on his business rounds. But instead of a stick he was holding a bugle in his hand and making use of it as if it were a stick. This gesture of his attracted the people's attention. They began to murmur that, perhaps, such strange gestures are the causes of the success of this successful trader. Others supported this thought.

Now there was a sensation in this 'city of blind followers'. Everybody left his or her work and rushed to purchase a bugle and all the bugles were sold out within no time. Then the old trader met the foreigner to ascertain his reaction. When he learnt that all bugles were sold out he advised him to leave the city as soon as possible because the following day the situation was going to be different.

The next morning the old trader with a bent waist went around the city with his usual supporting stick instead of the bugle. People repented over their folly and understood that they had followed him quite blindly and that neither the stick was the cause of success nor the bugle.

In the words of Rumi: Imitating them has ruined me.

A thousand damnations on such imitation.

Just as it is essential for an individual to carve his own path and polish his personality so it is necessary for a successful society to proceed on new highways and never beat the old paths blindly. Otherwise a society cannot prosper.

Some ignorant people of our society are under the impression, (due to misguiding propaganda) that the secret of success in the field of industry attained by the west is due to their distance from religion and morality. They imagine that the reason of west's superiority over the east is due to dancing, singing and the nudity of their women. Owing to their sense of inferiority some such people want to become like the westerners by copying their dress and adopting their attires. They fail to understand that it is the style of an industrialized society.

The foundation of their progress is knowledge and research. The base of their civilization is that they are not subservient to any super power. They are standing on their own feet as independent nations and are constantly occupied in scientific research.

Here it is befitting to remember Iqbal Lahori's lofty thoughts and show our gratitude to him by quoting some of his couplets, which are full of wisdom:

Avoid Blind Following

The blind imitation of the west makes the east forget its position.

In fact the eastern nations should have criticized the dancing of veilless women.

The strength of the west is neither owing to the colorful faces of girls nor due to their bare legs.

Nor it has sprung from their haircut.

The stability of the west is also not Latin script.

There is no relation between power, hat, suit and Latin script. Eastern headdress never comes in the way of science and literature.

The strength of the Firangis is due to science and industry. Their lamp is burning with the knowledge and industry.

O witty and senseless youth!

You must concentrate on knowledge not on the dress of the westerners.

The path of progress requires nothing except an eye for knowledge.

This or that kind of a cap or a hat has nothing to do with progress.

It is enough if you want to be knowledgeable and intelligent.

It is enough if you have an appetite for knowledge and an enthusiasm for it.

The societies, which are wonderstruck and awed by the west take refuge under their hats and suits instead of breaking the hands of oppressive super powers and instead of lighting up their own paths of life with the lamps of knowledge.

Unless a community has its own educational and economic system it cannot make any important advance.

We have with us an educational and research institute named Daar Al Funoon since the year 1269 Hijri era. It was founded by a very wise and courageous Iranian scholar the late Mirza Mir Taqvi Khan Amir Kabir.

The so called superpowers felt that the Iranian nation has adopted a new path and intends to proceed on lines, which were not selected by others till then. Then before long the people on the payroll

Avoid Blind Following

of oppression and imperialism got him murdered in a bath of Kashan city. More than a hundred years have passed therefrom but there is no educational institution to match the one founded by him.

Shahryar a well known modern poet, has expressed his thoughts regarding educational courses in this manner:

Our educational courses are only increasing ignorance because they wants us to believe that we are well of whereas it is not so.

It does not provide a single lesson to the youth.

It makes him recite things like a parrot without any use.

Those schools must shut down which open doors of disgrace for the community.

Beware that the aliens' music is but a lullaby to keep us in deep sleep.

The loss resulting from an institution, which ruins the first part of your age, is that you will have to seek knowledge again from the starting point.

Moreover another six years will be required for building up interest in it.

It won't by incorrect if the vice chancellor of our university tells us today that, "Our Inter passed pupils do not know Persian and if they do not know Persian then, definitely, they do not know anything."

A community made up of imitators who, instead of thinking independently, always rely on others is like a herd of sheep wherein all the animals blindly follow the first sheep. If you put a hurdle of stick before the first one so that it may jump over it, all the animals would follow suit. Then even if you remove that barrier they would continue to jump at that point.

It is said that a leader of an area called 'Fiji' was once traveling through a mountainous terrain. A group of men was also following him. By chance the leader fell down. Seeing this all the followers also threw themselves on the ground. Only one man remained standing. He criticized all others for this unwise imitation.

You will be surprised to know that all the people criticized that person asking him whether he knew better than the leader?

Our great Divine Book the Holy Quran has bitterly criticized blind following and reliance on others.

Avoid Blind Following

The progeny of Hazrat Ibrahim (a.s.) had, for a long time, remained the torchbearer of Monotheism and struggled against idol-worship. But, thereafter, as a consequence of incorrect following, they had worshipped idols made of wood and metal for several centuries. They turned the Holy Kaaba, which was the center of monotheism into the abode of idols named Laat and Uzza.

It so happened that one of their leaders in the course of his journey was impressed by some idol-worshipping people and he also brought an idol for himself and kept it with him. In this way a monotheist community became influenced by him due to blind imitation.

Of course what we mean by 'blind following' is the wrong and harmful following. Otherwise if Taqlid (imitation or following) means the approach of an ignorant man to a wise one and of a layman to an expert, then that approach is certainly not bad. Rather it is considered as the basis of life in advanced communities. A sick man goes to a doctor, one who wants something to be done goes to the relevant workman and they accept what the expert says.

Secrets of Success

The Tale of a Stupid Sufi

Many dervishes lived in a Khanqah (convent). They were all penniless. Per chance another dervish came there in the course of his journey back home. He entrusted his donkey to the watchman of the monastery and entered therein intending to pass the night with the resident saints.

The hungry saints were pleased to see the newcomer. They held a meeting and hatched a plot, justifying in the following manner: "As the dervishes of this Khanqah are half-dead due to hunger and as Islam allows eating of a dead corpse too in such hard times, it would be permissible to sell out the donkey of this new dervish."

All agreed to this and they sold out the ass of that newcomer without his knowledge. Then they filled their bellies with food purchased from the price of that donkey. After the feast they also arranged a singing and dancing party. The traveler too joined the group. The singer opened his song with the words: "The ass is gone.'

The drummer beat his drum and cried 'the ass is gone, the ass is gone'. Everyone in the party sang these words with such zeal and enthusiasm that following them, the newcomer traveler too started

Avoid Blind Following

clapping and singing, 'the ass is gone, the ass is gone'.

This repetition of 'the ass is gone' continued till dawn. The owner of the ass also sang these words happily with others.

The dervishes vacated the Khanqah next morning and all went away to their homes. The ass-owner came out and asked for his ass from the gatekeeper.

He said, "The hungry dervishes had prepared their food last night by selling out your ass and you too had participated in the feast."

Then he added, "I was helpless. The Sufis had overpowered me and I was almost dead. You were yourself among them and now you are asking their whereabouts?"

The poor dervish retorted, "Why did you not inform me about this mischief? Now to whom should I complain? Which court shall I approach?"

The watchman responded, "By God! I wanted to inform you but when I entered the Khanqah and saw that you too were taking part in the party and singing 'the ass is gone, the ass is gone' more enthusiastically than others, I thought that surely you were aware of the event, otherwise it was not becoming for dervish like you to sing anything without purpose."

The poor dervish replied, "Seeing that all were singing the song, I also liked it and I too began to sing. Now this is the evil consequence of that blind following. A hundred condemnations on such following. What is the use of blind following people who sold their character for food?"

Today the communities, which are awed by the West and become mad of their industrial progress, have lost their identity so badly that, it seems, they never had any civilization and culture and arts and sciences of their own!

People are adopting useless ways of the West and that too in the matter of clothing and manners as if their personality is identified only with these things.

In this connection Maulavi Mir Hadi says:

Knowledge, wisdom, intelligence and religion are not connected with dress and cap and turban etc. of the Maulavi. In fact man becomes sophisticated due to his knowledge and manners. No one can become sophisticated by just wearing a particular suit and hat.

Counsel

Electricity is generated by the contact of positive and negative wires. Similarly progress too is achieved with the confluence of two streams of thoughts. Sometimes consultation lights up the future path for man and sometimes it brightens up a vast horizon.

Of course, consultation never means that man should submit himself totally to others because it would also result in a loss like blind following which is a kind of suicide as it would only mean the assassination of one's intelligence and noble feelings. Consultation means that man may ask for the solution of his problems from others and may follow their advice or counsel after giving it full thought.

At the time of the battle of Khandaq (Trench) the huge army of the Arab polytheists advanced toward Medina to attack the Muslims. The Holy Prophet (s.a.w.a.) constituted a consultative committee of some experts in warfare. An experienced Persian companion, Salman Farsi suggested digging of a three meter wide and two meter deep ditch on the outskirts of the town and a trough at a distance of every hundred feet and posting strong warriors entrusted with the responsibility of defending the ditch front to prevent the enemy from approaching it and to drive them away, if necessary, by raining arrows and even stones on them.

The advice of Salman was liked by the Holy Prophet as well as by his companions and the work of ditch digging was completed in 25 days. The enemy soldiers were astonished to see this innovative military strategy. They had to camp for about a month and return empty handed after suffering the loss of some soldiers.

In the modern world states are governed by consultative councils and senates. Most unfortunate and extremely mean is the nation, which remains under the influence of a big oppressive power and entrusts the reins of its destiny to an individual.

Seeking counsel is one of the basic teachings of Islam. Allah Almighty ordains His Holy Prophet (s.a.w.a.): *(O Muhammad!) Consult your friends in social and political affairs.*

The Holy Prophet was in the heat of the battle of Badr. The enemies far exceeded in numbers and also had modern and devastating arms and were bent upon wiping out Islam altogether. The Holy Prophet arranged a high level meeting of war experts, then he turned towards the people and said, "Let me have your opinion in the matter of fighting with the

Quraish in this desert land. Is it advisable to go ahead to confront the enemy or should we return to Medina from here only?"

A companion named 'Miqdad' stood up and said, "Our hearts are with you. We will never tell you what Bani Israel had told to Musa (a.s.). When he had invited them to wage jihad the Bani Israel had replied: O Musa! You and your God may go ahead and fight. We will sit here. But we say: O Muhammad (s.a.w.a.)! You and your Allah may proceed further for war. We are also with you."

Another companion from the Ansars, Saad bin Maaz, got up and pointing toward the Red Sea said: "O great leader! If you fling into this sea, we also will jump into it following you faithfully. None of us will ever turn his face from your honor. We are not at all afraid of the enemy. Perhaps we may, in this path, render services which might please you."

Other companions also liked the opinions of these two companions. The Islamic army got motivated. Thus the Holy Prophet (s.a.w.a.) made up his mind to move and march forward. Through such consultation he created a fresh feeling in his army and ordered to march forward.

The Holy Prophet took such advice not only in this holy war but he did similarly on other occasions also like the battle of Uhad and the war at Khaibar and obtained good results.

Young people should gain from the experience of the seniors as they have seen the ups and downs of life. It is likely that, due to inexperience, we may look only at the apparent aspects and remain unaware of the consequences.

The reason of great victories achieved during the days of the second caliph was 'Consultation'.

The caliph of the time used to put his problems before Amirul Mo-mineen Ali (a.s.) who, in the light of his intelligence, used to tell the secrets of success in battles.

When the caliph of the time asked the opinion of Ali (a.s.) in the matter of fighting against the Sasanids and said, "If you so advise, I may participate in this battle myself."

Amirul Mo-mineen replied, "In case the Muslims are defeated they will not have any shelter if you also go to war with the army. But if you remain in the Islamic capital, you will be able to send help if needed. Thus the people will have a refuge."

History is the Best Teacher

We are fortunate because we are not the first ones to arrive in this world. The sky above us has seen the lives of millions of human beings on this planet through the everobserving eyes of the star. Those people saw happiness and sorrow, brightness and darkness, love and hatred. They indulged in war and peace. In short, they saw thousands of aspects of human life.

Though, prior to us, many people went to their graves taking the secrets of their success with them without revealing them to others and they have been forgotten, yet different parts of the earth and apparently the silent deserted lands and the ruined structures have preserved noteworthy aspects of their lives for us and writers have noted them down for our benefit. Thus this world has become a great training school for us.

We obtain several lessons by studying the pages of history, by researching the lives of men in various parts of the world and by pondering over ancient remnants and can thus become wiser like our elders.

Is it not so that the product of a whole life is only a little 'experience'?

Does history not make us conversant with the best of experiences? Is not human history a mirror showing the past people in their entirety? The misfortunes and mistake as well as the victories and reasons thereof are clearly seen in this mirror.

In the Holy Quran, the last edition of Divine Guidance for mankind, we find this ordinance of studying the life of past communities. We have been asked to take lessons from the special aspects of their lives.

The commander of the believers, Ali (a.s.) says, "O My son! Though I did not myself live with the people of the past yet I have studied their history thoroughly and attentively. Thus I have been aware of the ups and downs of their time and I know the relevant laws. I have comprehended their history so perfectly that, it seems I were living among them."

History is the best guide for the present generation. Teaching history is much more difficult then teaching physics and chemistry. There are some formulas by which the teacher can teach these subjects nicely. But in case of history it is necessary to think deeply, make research and strive hard to reach the conclusion. Until history teachers do not get themselves satisfied regarding these requirements they cannot fulfill their obligation and cannot get the desired results. On this basis everyone who knows history cannot be called a historian.

A point, which is more minute than a hair, is that everyone who does not shave off his hair cannot be considered a sage.

We must make efforts to understand the secrets and truths of history. Otherwise it is no use just reading it or only memorizing it. Secrets and truths of history are those bitter medicines which man can obtain with much difficulty. Man can cure both individual and collective ailments by using those medicines.

It is incumbent upon everyone, especially upon the administrators and other managers, to make deep study and research in the history of England, history of the great revolution of France, and, especially the history of Islam and of the last part of the rule of Banu Umayyah and the revolution of the Abbasids and ascertain the causes of the failures of those who had ruled over the masses for centuries.

As a principle we should cultivate within us a zeal for reading books because it raises the level of thinking, strengthens the mind and offers the treasures of great people free to those who can obtain it. Today the standard of a nation's progress is measured and its culture weighed by the use of paper by that community. It is said that in Switzerland, which is understood to be the cradle of civilization, taking into consideration its population, the quantity of paper used is much more than any other country. Experts have confirmed that paper used in Tehran is more than the paper utilized by all other provinces of Iran collectively.

Today it can be ascertained how many books are published in a year in a country and how many copies are printed in each edition. It is also calculated how many people benefit from the public libraries in a particular country.

In this way it is determined how much the level of public thinking has risen during the past year and how did it fare compared to other nations.

Secrets of authors are always hidden somewhere in their books. Once when Aristotle intended to publish his book Alexander put a hindrance so as to prevent others from reaching the level of his teacher's accomplishments.

During the medieval centuries the Popes and Clergy had established an 'educational society' and had prevented the general public from reading books so that they (the clergy) might make maximum earnings from the ignorance of the masses and may continue to have total control on them.

A good book adorns morality, builds up the personality and teaches the secrets of life. However useless books should be discarded as harmful books impair ones intelligence.

A wise man has said, "Let me know what you are reading, so that I may tell you what you are."

Shouphenhauer has said, "Life is more precious than the time spent in reading useless books."

We must spare some time every day for reading useful books that increase our knowledge and we must consider the book as our best friend. There is no friend in the world better than a book. No one is more sympathetic than a good book in this house of sorrow. In moments of solitude there are thousands of bounties in the company of a book and not a single hardship.

Making Use of Opportunities

People do get enough opportunities and time but they do not take the advantage of this golden key to success and miss the chance due to procrastination. One should not only complete today's work today but if possible also do the next day's work today.

Once Abu Muslim Khurasani was asked, "What is the secret of your success?"

His response was, "I have never postponed today's work for tomorrow."

Sometimes it also so happens that energy spent in postponing a job proves enough for finishing the same work.

Some students who are not allowed to appear in the March- April examinations and who have to appear in October-November take the maximum advantage of this time and opportunity whereas some waste their time in repenting and in meaningless thoughts until the time of examination arrives. Such pupils not only face failure they also retreat a few steps backward. Some people only shed tears on the past and say:

"Had we purchased that garden we would have a earned much benefit. Had we enrolled in this university we would have become among the VIPs of the country today… "

Such people waste all their time in repenting and shedding tears on 'yesterday's grave', though, if even now, they become wise and restart their jobs they can fulfill all, or at least, some of their aspirations. But they continue to cry on spilt milk.

You cannot repurchase time that is spent. Hence it is better not to sell it in the first place as time is a precious pearl.

Some people have the opposite nature. They think of the future but their worry is so much that in that anxiety, they are unable to do anything during the time that is at their disposal. We have seen students who are always afraid of being debarred from appearing in the examination and who keep on saying, "We are afraid our year will be wasted, we may not be allowed to sit in the examination."

Such restlessness does not allow them to work and study and they lose the opportunity. How meaningful is this Arabic couplet:

Whatever time is gone is gone and what will come has not yet come so get up and take the maximum benefit of what is in between the two nonexistent moments.

O Saadi! Yesterday has passed away and the forthcoming tomorrow does not now exist. Hence appreciate the time between the two.

Youth is the Most Opportune Time

Youth is the best time for working, learning and earning. The greatest opportunity in ones life is the youth. A young man is like the mountaineer who has reached the top of Himalayas and is full of joy. He has passion, aspiration, hope, zeal and ardor for work. He has numerous capabilities for inventing things. After some years these physical and spiritual powers begin to decrease. Nerves become weak, eyesight becomes feeble, and capacities lessen.

The Master of the Pious, Ali (a.s.) says, "Man understands the importance of his youth and health after losing them."

The Holy Prophet (s.a.w.a.) had given many admonitions to his great companion, Abu Zar. One of them was, "Realize the importance of your youth before the advent of your old age."

A young branch is the adornment of a garden. When it becomes old the gardener pulls it out and throws it away. A young branch produces a new fruit for every flower and the old branch is destined to wither away.

The great and successful people never repent over the past. At the same time no anxiety regarding the future prevents them from performing their jobs at the appropriate time.

Almighty God has given a natural wisdom to every man, which, increases with the passing of age. But, in addition to this natural wisdom, in the light of knowledge and experiments, we also get a sort of acquired wisdom. This acquired wisdom, in fact fosters the natural wisdom and raises it to perfection.

Suppose we have two trees of pistachio. Both are capable of giving nine kilo pistachio. But if we provide fertilizer to one of them, the treated plant would produce twice the pistachios.

Only those people are successful who always and in all available opportunities, be it childhood, youth or old age, polish their natural brainpower or intelligence with the acquired knowledge. And the best time for doing so is youth.

The Holy Prophet of Islam (s.a.w.a.) has said, "Opportunities pass away like the clouds of spring. Success is the right of a farmer who takes advantage of it."

Those who have valued their time and age never waste their life in futile works. Some scholars have written their books during hours, which are not appreciated by the common people.

For example, Dr. Mardun Cud wrote one of his famous books during the time he got while traveling from one patient's house to the other's.

Dr. Borni learned French and Italian languages during the time he got while commuting to his office and back.

The great scholar, the late Mudarris Khayabani had written one of his famous books regarding Persian synonyms during refreshment breaks.

Napoleon had defeated the enemy in the event of 'Arikula' with the help of only 25 companions because the opponent was tired and Napoleon took the advantage of this opportunity and was victorious despite having lesser men.

Some people waste their life and time as if they are the enemies of their own lives and times. Today there are many pastimes that provide less recreation and waste more time.

Of course, tired nerves do require rest and recreation. One should never think that recreation is a waste of time. Because, lacking a stroll, breathing fresh air, viewing beautiful scenes, participating in joyful meetings and all such things give respite to our nerves from tension and add vigor to life.

But at the same time we should not squander our precious life by imagining that every vain and futile pastime is recreation.

Today's youth mostly turns to television, cinema and magazines for recreation. They should realize that every film is not worth viewing. Nor is every book pleasing, educational, instructive and advantageous.

Crime, horror and sex films are not worthy of appreciation.

Rather they turn youth into untimely old age.

Firm Determination

Man, like other animals, also has the power of 'determination'. In other animals it is controlled by their beastly nature, whereas man's determination or will must be in control of his brain or wisdom.

In this chapter on determination we do not intend to say that we must hand over the reins of our will or wish in the hands of passionate desires and perform every deed according to beastly nature. In that case we will not rank above an animal and thus will lose our status.

Here our aim is that after giving proper thought if we come to a conclusion that such and such work is beneficial or desirable and that it should be done then we should make a decision to do it and should remain firm on that decision to the best of our ability. We must realize that the more the hardship or difficulty in any work the more is the demand to be firm and unflinching for its performance. Here the secret of success is firm decision or strong will. It removes difficulties and obstacles from the path.

The demeanor and the facial appearance of great people give an idea of their unyielding and firm determination, which pours success on them.

Men with firm decision are always respected in every strata of the society. Others cannot harm them. But people having a weak will power wander like stray dogs and are so frail and shaky that the enemy overcomes them easily.

Reluctance and hesitation is disastrous for success and it is a clear sign of moral debility. Indecision inflicts a fatal blow to carefulness and higher intelligence.

Alexander the Great had said, "One of the secrets of my victories is my strong will. After making a decision I do not like to hesitate in carrying it out."

Timurlane, Napoleon and Nadir Shah were among the recognized military commanders. They used to delay their decisions but after making a decision they never changed it.

A man with a firm decision is like a soldier on duty who has already received alert orders. Such a man bears all circumstances and no hindrance can block his path. The difficulties in the path leading to his goal are unable to make anything appear impossible in his eyes.

Goethe says, "A man with firm decision and strong will can change the world to his liking."

Firm Determination

In the war of Qudisiyah, the commander-in-chief of the Persian army, Farrukhzaad called a delegate from the commander of the Muslim army. The Muslim commander, Saad bin Waqqas, sent Rabe bin Amir as his representative. The strong will of this Bedouin Arab made Rustom spellbound.

When he arrived in the court of Rustom, he saw that Rustom was sitting on a golden throne and rich carpets were spread on the floor with gold-threaded pillows on them.

Such deceptive things never awe a man with firm decision and strong will. His determination did not flinch at all that pomp.

When he arrived near Rustom he did not alight from his horse, rather he pushed his animal forward and entered Rustom's stable in a mounted position. When the servants of Rustom tried to stop him he retorted, "You had invited a delegate from us. I am the representative of the Muslims. If you do not want to see me I will go back."

Then slowly and silently, with complete ease and seriousness, he approached the throne of Rustom. Walking over the pompous carpets he went forward and sat down on the floor. Then said, "We are not accustomed to such luxury."

When the interpreter of Rustom asked him why the Muslim army had attacked he replied, "Allah Almighty has put a responsibility on us that we should release God's slaves from all sorts of oppressions and from the evils of other religions and invite them to abide by and accept the just law of Islam. If they accept our invitation we have no enmity toward them.

Otherwise we will fight with them and will either kill or be killed. Either way we reach paradise."

Observing such a strong determination of this Bedouin, Rustom who was struck with awe, said, "Give us some time for corresponding and consulting our elders."

"We can give you three days. More delay is not advisable," said the Muslim representative.

Rustom said, "It seems you are the commander and thus you intend to sign a treaty with us."

He replied, "No. I am merely a member of the Muslim society. Of course all the Muslims are limbs of a single body. If any one of them gives shelter to others, all the Muslims are bound to concur with it."

The Commander of the Faithful, Ali (a.s.) Orders His Son to Have Firm Determination

The Battle of Camel was fought between Hazrat Ali (a.s.) and the breakers of the treaty. For making an attack in this war Amirul Mo-mineen (a.s.) had given the flag to his dear son, Muhammad Hanafiyah and to fortify his determination he advised, "Even if the mountains around Basra give way, you should not budge from your place, to retreat. Lighten your teeth. Offer your head on loan to Allah. Keep your eye on the last rows of the army. Close your eyes for seeing any adversity and remove difficulties with the special strength of your firm will. Understand that the final victory is in the hands of Allah. Our responsibility is only to fight in the way as shown by Him."

The Amirul Mo-mineen sent one of his commanders (Malik Ashtar) as the governor of Egypt. In his letter addressed to the people of Egypt, Ali (a.s) had praised his emissary thus:

"O people of Egypt! I have sent to you a slave from among the slaves of Allah towards you. He does not sleep during the hours of danger. He does not fear the enemy in time of peril. For evildoers he is more devastating than fire...He is one of the swords of Allah, which does not blunt nor it misses its hit."

We can benefit from the precious pearls hidden beneath the ground of our intelligence, wisdom and alertness only if we have an unbreakable determination. Man can advance only in the light of his steel-like will.

What is self-confidence? Only that man may take a decision in the light of his brainpower and then act accordingly. He may regard himself able to perform that task and refrain from those matters, which can weaken his will.

People, who have toured the entire world, possessed positive thinking and who had founded educational institutions and industries had removed the words like 'impossible' from the vocabulary of their lives. They viewed everything from the angle of 'feasible' and 'I can'. A man having negative thoughts and weak will not only loses the benefit from advantageous opportunities but he also becomes a hindrance in the way of others. He wastes his life in disallowing his inner potentiality and in creating roadblocks for himself.

One of the motives of strengthening the will is love for our aim and zeal in work. First of all man must try to cultivate interest and zeal for his work. Awake or asleep, he must always dream of his work. This

Firm Determination

should continue until his mind is occupied with that issue every moment.

The gigantic pyramids of Egypt, the lofty palaces of the czars, sky-high mansions, and multi-volume books are the results of unbreakable intention.

The expertise of Russians and Americans in astronomy is skyrocketing only due to their strong will.

Weak willed people are like papers flowing on the surface of the sea. They have no strength of their own. But men with firm determination are like expert swimmers who, with the power of their will and determination, rip the water currents and proceed in the direction of their choice.

Napoleon used to say, "The word, 'impossible' should be removed from the dictionary of life." He used to become very unhappy on hearing words and like 'cannot be done', 'I cannot do' and 'I do not know'. He used to say, "Just desire and it will be done."

Nowadays many ailments are treated by strengthening ones will power. Many difficulties become easy before a firm determination.

Secrets of Success

In the words of Hafiz Shirazi: There are many dangers in the way to Laila's house. For taking the first step it is necessary that you should be Majnoon.

Awareness of Circumstances

Before starting any work it is necessary to understand the conditions and demands of the atmosphere and then to draw a program accordingly. Jobs done without first studying the relevant trends often end up in failure.

Imam Ja'far Sadiq (a.s.) said, "One who becomes aware of the conditions of his times is saved from a sudden attack."

This is a very valuable principle. Had the Muslims and other backward communities of the world, paid attention to this rule in the matter of politics they would never have been subdued by the invaders. Many misfortunes are the result of ignorance of and carelessness toward prevailing conditions.

In western Rome Before the advent of Islam, there was no progress at all in arts and science, trade and industry and military affairs, because the people there were so unmindful of the world that when the Muslim army besieged Constantinople their wise men were discussing vain issues as: Can some angel accommodate them on the point of a needle?

History repeats itself. Muslims also fell to such idleness at a time when they were at the peak of their progress and advancement. The eastern states, particularly the heads of Islamic countries were pitiably unaware of the conditions of their masses. They woke up only after the west took control of all sciences and industries.

Even the recurring defeat of the Ottoman Empire did not awaken its rulers. The rulers remained in sleep even after being defeated by the Europeans. Suddenly when they saw enemy planes roaring over their heads they began to open their eyes wide with astonishment.

They could not imagine that it was the work of human beings. Perhaps they were thinking that the flying machines were the handiworks of angels!

The nineteenth century was very important from the view-point of discoveries and inventions. But in those days Iran was engaged in internal struggles. Those responsible for such state of affairs were in deep sleep. They were unaware of the conditions of the world.

For example it would not be out of place to mention here that during the reign of Fatehali Shah, Napoleon wanted to conquer India. He intended to snatch away that fertile land from the hands of the British East India Company. In this connection, in order to obtain the support of Iranian public and government, he wrote a letter to the Shah of Iran.

Awareness of Circumstances

Strangely enough they could not find anyone in the court of the Shah of Iran who could translate the letter of Napoleon for the king.

It was considered inadvisable to get it translated from the embassies of other countries. They were thus compelled to send that letter to the Iranian embassy in Baghdad where there was a French-knowing person who translated it.

Such a dosing nation cannot preserve its political, economical and cultural independence and it has to live under the obligation of others.

A great Iranian poet has given vent to his burning feelings in this connection thus:

We are the ones who had collected tax from kings, then we took away their belt and crown.

We took their royal cap and their throne, which was decorated with pearls and ivory.

We emptied their treasures.

We did not fear storms and high-speed winds.

We were a dreaded topic in China and other countries. Egypt and Oman were awed by our glory.

Our power was obvious in Spain and Rome. Granada and Ashbila used to obey us.

Saqliya was under our flag.

Royal decree was our sign, which used to cover everything under the sun.

These couplets pertain to the era when Muslims and Iranians were awake. It can be said that the East was proud of the glorious past of the Islamic world. But what is our condition today? The same poet describes:

Alas! This field has been destroyed by flood. The afflicted farmer went into deep sleep.

The blood of our heart took the color of wine. The heat of fever burnt down our body.

The cool face turned into a burning one.

The eyes of intelligence too got covered with blood. The wealth went away and health turned to illness.

Institution of the Pope

The Pope's grand institution, after a long duration of oppressive rule, got disintegrated, because it had tried to remain in power by creating a cruel court called Inquisition. But it had erred seriously and was unaware of the changes, which had already taken place in the masses. Those changes in the thoughts of the people tended to destroy the wrong thoughts of the clergy and the priests. The church took no notice of those changing trends at all. It was of the opinion that it would be able to stem the flood with the help of oppression, use of force and torture. But this thinking was merely the result of their ignorance of the change in winds. If it had not, at the last moments of its life, prepared a new plan and had it not adapted itself to the new age, no sign of Christianity would have remained in the world today. It cleared its sleepy eyes, changed its course, started schools, colleges and universities and regained its past position through educational service to the society.

The Most Intelligent Man of the East

In the nineteenth century, an ordinary but a very intelligent person (Amir Kabir) rose up. He felt that the misfortune of the easterners was due to the changes, which had taken place in the west. Those changes had created a vast gulf between the people of the east and the west. So long as that gap was not filled the western communities would continue to monopolize Iran.

So he studied the circumstances carefully and realized that it was not the time to fight with swords and arrows. Modern technology has changed the method of production. Gas and steam have subdued all material treasures.

Therefore, Amir Kabir, in 1849 AD (1266 HE) established an institution named 'Daral Funoon' (House of Arts & Science). The eastern wing of this institute was completed by the end of the year 1267.

They deputed a reliable person to Vienna who requested the Emperor of Austria to send a commander of infantry, a tutor of artillery, a teacher of mounted police, an expert of mining, two miners, a professor of medicine and surgery and a pharmacist for five or six years and paid each of them a monthly salary of 4000 Tomans.

But alas! Traitors of the nation came forward to put off this shining lamp and Amir Kabir was killed at the hands of the butchers of Qachar a few years after the establishment of Daral Funoon in the year 1268.

Observing closely the trends of the world, Amir Kabir had realized that a major cause of the backwardness of Iran and other counties was that their economy depended on the west. Iran had become a market of the west-manufactured materials and was only their consumer.

Awareness of Circumstances

This reliance on the west, rather helplessness and beggary, had destroyed the capabilities of Iranians. The Iranis had become only the suppliers of raw material to the industries of the west. They were pulling on their days like a daily-waged laborer. Amir put at the disposal of the artist enough capital for the expansion of manufacturing industries.

He established sugar factories in Saari, rope and cloth in Tehran, silk in Kashan and Horse-carriages in Isfahan etc. He

gave much assistance to cloth manufacturers in Isfahan and Kashan, encouraged many experts for preparing new things and making inventions and had also arranged an exhibition of Iranian products in Iran.

All these services rendered by Amir Kabir were the result of his awareness about the existing trends and circumstances.

When roads were built in Iran and automobiles started rolling thereon, the joyful journeys on horseback and in horse and donkey carts came to an end. The carriers of mulelitters began to complain so much that, strangely enough, they even asked the government to cancel the licenses of pannier-owners! All this was the consequence of remaining unaware of the happenings in the world.

Sometimes our businessmen do things, which are disliked by people in today's world. In fact such deeds of theirs are like waging war against progress. As a result they meet with sure defeat.

Here we become convinced of the importance of a great religious leader's words who said: Do not fight with time otherwise time will fight with you.

Enemy: A Stepstone to Success

Only he is victorious who has recognized the world fully and who considers his enemy as the first step toward victory.

Intelligent people think that the enemy teaches him how to march towards success, because, the adversary is the best type of mirror with reflects our defects through pen or tongue. It decreases our pride and arrogance and, sometimes, helps in uplifting our hidden abilities.

The advances of the east and the west are the consequence of competition. If competitions come to end, capabilities would not flower. Thus, if there were no struggle between individuals or masses the progress in new inventions too would become stagnant.

Failure is a Ladder to Success

One of the secrets of success is that we should not fear failures. Rather, we must pick up the sweet fruits hidden in defeat. Failure is like a mirror, which shows us our weaknesses and defects accurately.

Great and wise people consider failure as a bridge to victory. They endeavor to see that the causes of failure are not repeated. In fact they do not consider failure as defeat. What they really fear is that they should never be disheartened or demoralized.

History shows that many victories came after defeats. It is so because the failed person enters the field again with a new determination and spirit and achieves success as he is convinced that the distance between success and failure is very less.

Those who fail but do not get disappointed are the ones to give up so easily. They continue to march forward gradually with a strong will and rest only after reaching their goal.

In the battle of Uhad, Muslims had to taste defeat due to an act of disobedience. But that defeat was so educative that it cleared the road to future success.

Secrets of Success

Napoleon says, "I have seen so many defeats that I have now learnt how to defeat the enemy."

And what an apt statement is made by someone else: For those with weak spirit defeat is a fatal poison but for powerful souls it is a ladder to success.

In the Islamic Law, despair is considered a great sin. An apparent effect of defeat is disappointment but since the days of old people have said: The brightness of dawn comes after the end of a dark night.

It is also said that sometimes hope remains hidden behind hopelessness and disappointment. Hope follows hopelessness.

The great Iranian military commander Nadir Shah was determined to conquer Baghdad after capturing Kirmanshah from the Turks. He also conquered Samarrah, Kerbala, Najaf and some other towns of Iraq and then besieged Baghdad. But very soon, Topal Shah reached there with eighty thousand selected warriors to break the siege.

That army of the Ottoman Turks was armed with heavy artillery and numerically too they were more than the Iranians. During the fighting the horse of Nadir Shah was hit by an arrow, which drowned that animal in blood. The Iranian soldiers imagined that Nadir Shah was killed so they disintegrated and anarchy spread. When Nadir Shah saw this he ordered retreat. Nearly 30,000 Iranians and 20,000 Turks fell in this battle. The Turks took control of the entire artillery and arms of the Iranians. Nadir Shah reached Mandali with surviving soldiers most of whom did not even have shoes on.

In the eyes of the ordinary people this defeat has finished the Iranian army. But what gave salvation to Nadir shah was that he did not accept defeat, as his spirit was till alive. After returning to Hamadan, he collected fighters from all over Iran and prepared a fresh army within two months. There were at least 2,00,000 men it. Then he went to Kirmanshah. From there he went to Karkook and gave a severe defeat to the Turkish army. Then he surrounded Baghdad once more and compelled the Turkish warriors to surrender. As a consequence the Turkish government had to promise that all the Persian lands would be returned to Iran within ten years.

The Persian King Plucks Sweet Fruit from a Sour Tree

Behram Shah was very fond of hunting. But he was totally unaware of the conditions of his people. He used to become pleased merely by seeing his well-managed military and the flattering talks of his courtiers. He knew nothing about innocent prisoners languishing in his jails.

In such circumstances a war broke out on the borders of Iran. The king was compelled to ask help from the people. But they did not pay any attention to his call and did not cooperate with him, as he had not cared for them. The king was shocked to see this. He began to think about the reasons of his helplessness before his masses. He realized that there was some irregularity in the government administration, which he did not know, and that irregularity had turned the people against the regime.

One day, he went out of the city in disguise. There he suddenly saw that a man had hung the skin of a dog in front of his tent. The King of Iran went forward, said Salam to that person, introduced himself as a traveler and asked the reason for hanging the dog skin. After much persuasion the man replied, "I was maintaining myself with the help of some sheep that used to graze in this greenery. This skin is of a dog, which used to guard them. My shepherd and I were hopefully thinking of expanding our work. But after a few days the shepherd came and informed me that wolves had taken away a sheep. He brought similar sad news for two or three days continuously. So I became suspicious about the dog. Then the shepherd and I kept a vigil on the dog for a whole night. We observed that the dog had cultivated sexual relations with a female and his passion had allowed the wolves to attack our herd. So we have hung its skin here that people may understand that such is the end of those who accept a responsibility and then show dishonesty in their duty.

This story shocked the king who told himself, "Perhaps, the reason of my failure is that I had over confidence in my courtiers." Thereafter he personally contacted different sections of the public without informing the yes-men of the court. He found that the unhappy people were not allowed even to complain and that a number of innocent people were imprisoned for not paying 'illegal' taxes.

He instantly brought about a kind of basic revolution. He transferred his courtiers, ministers and officers, punished the oppressors and thus regained the confidence of his masses. Soon thereafter he began to get support from all the sections of the society.

The Defeat of Hitler

Hitler had met defeat in the way Napoleon had suffered defeat. Napoleon had marched to conquer

Moscow in a severe winter. So he could not succeed and this thoughtless gesture proved to be the cause of his downfall. Had Hitler learnt a lesson from Napoleon's defeat he would not have repeated his mistake. Hitler invaded Russia in the scorching heat of summer on the 2nd June of 1941. He also saw almost what Napoleon had seen. Initially the German forces got some success and the allies had to retreat. Germans pursued them but thereafter the Germans had to suffer many difficulties in surrounding cities like Leningrad in a very hot season. Russians attacked them severely and the Germans were defeated.

Courage and Fearlessness

Courage, valor, fearlessness and boldness are all synonymous words. They are recognized as the basic qualities of a successful personality.

Surely, boldness is different from carelessness and haughtiness or impudence or rudeness. Similarly there is a vast difference between bravery and indiscipline.

Courage and fearlessness are the signs of manliness and in many tasks these qualities serve as a bridge to success. Rather no achievement, progress and advancement are attainable without courage and gallantry. All social and intellectual revolutions too require these qualities.

Fearful and timid people hide themselves in corners like birds retreat in cold season. They do not undertake any task for fear of their opponents. Such people neither become reputable nor can they bring any change in life. At the most they can remain in their original condition.

But bold and courageous people first realize the importance of their aim, ponder over every side of the matter, weigh probable profit or loss, prepare a program and then begin their job without caring for anything.

Here there is a difference between haughtiness and madness and courage and boldness. Careless people jump in without pondering over related matters. They do not keep an eye on their benefit or loss. Even if they prepare a program, wise people do not appreciate it. Such people are deceived by their strength and they take undue pride in themselves.

Here we can further clarify by giving an example from history.

After the passing away of the Holy Prophet (s.a.w.a), a person named Musailima Kazzab claimed to be a prophet in Oman.

The Muslim army went there to crush him. Musalima's men scattered away but he himself and some of his companions took shelter in a garden. That garden had four walls and it was situated in the midst of a castle. There was enough provision for four months in that fort.

The Muslim soldiers remained around the fort for some days but could not do anything. A meeting was held under the leadership of a famous commander Abu Dajana wherein, in the very beginning, it was decided that if Musailima were not captured at the end of the siege, the mischievous fellow would continue to mislead the people by his deceitful gestures and thus would prove to be great risk to Islam. So it would not be a matter of regret if some Muslims were martyred in an attempt to capture him. Then there was a discussion about the ways of arresting him. Abu Dajana said, "I want only ten persons who are ready to sacrifice their lives for this cause."

At once ten people came forward as volunteers. Then Abu Dajana said, "These ten persons including myself will, one by one, sit on a shield. Other soldiers will, with the help of their spears, raise that shield upward until the hand of the man sitting on the shield reached up to the wall of the castle. Thus when all reach the wall they will enter the castle with the help of ropes. First of all I will hold the rope and go inside and try to open the gates from inside. If my companions see that I am killed, another will follow. If he too is killed, the third man will get in. In this way, as a result of the self-sacrifice at least one person will reach the gate and open it for the Muslim army.

Per chance, Abu Dajana, himself achieved the task. He lowered a rope, entered the fort, fought for a while and succeeded in opening the gate. Thus the last center of corruption was destroyed with the capture and killing of Musailima Kazzab.

Had Abu Dajana not shown this courage, the Muslims would have never succeeded.

At the time of victory over Spain, Moosa bin Nasir, who was the commander of the Muslim arm in Africa, determined to capture Europe. He sent his slave Tariq bin Ziyad with a small group of people to Spain for spying.

When Tariq reached Spain and observed the enemy from every angle he understood that they were bent upon attacking the Muslims. Tariq thought that if he sends a report to his chief and awaits his response the enemy might become alert. So he ordered his men to burn down the ships in which they had reached the coast of Spain. When the ships began to burn, some took exception to that act and said, "You have made us shelter less by burning our ships. Now we cannot return to our homes."

Tariq replied, "The Muslim is not like a bird, which has a particular nest."

Then he got up, stood in the valley which today is known by the name of Gibraltar. Before his eyes the sea was roaring loudly. He delivered such a forceful speech that the audience could hear only his words even in the midst of the lashing of the ocean waves. The sea had, perhaps, become silent.

Tariq said, "Brother! The roaring sea is behind you and the army of the enemy in front of you. Your enemy has heaps of foodstuff and arms whereas you have only that which you can snatch from them with the strength of your hands. You do not have any armor except the swords hanging on your waists."

This forceful speech inspired much courage in the Muslim warriors. Their blood began to boil in fervor and they forced the enemy to surrender in a very short time as a result of their fearless fighting. Spain was conquered in this way.

The Courage of Martin Luther in Bringing about Religious Reform

Due to the fear of the Christian clergy the uneasiness of the masses could not be expressed by their tongues and they were feeling suffocated. No one dared to utter a single word of complain against the Pope and the clergy around him.

Martin Luther went to Rome in 1510 AD and saw for himself that those occupying high ranks in the church were careless in their duties regarding religion. So his determination to reform the religion doubled. Finally he put up a notification at the gate of the highest church informing the people that he had some points, which he wanted to discuss with knowledgeable persons.

Luther raised serious objections against the ways and manners of the religious leaders. He said that after becoming respectable in the eyes of the masses the priests claimed to get people's sins pardoned. Martin said this gesture of the priests was a kind of misappropriation.

The clergy became very angry at this criticism. They warned Martin to refrain from his undesirable propaganda. But he took no notice of their threats and continued voice his criticism in public meetings.

The Vatican was then compelled to declare that Martin had become unbeliever. Martin burnt the Pope's edict in public and took shelter with Frederick the third. Yet he continued his mission and at last, as a result of his courage he rested only after separating some wrong things of Christianity from religion and founded the Protestant order.

The examples quoted by us so far were related to courage in social affairs. But you can find many events of boldness in individual and personal matters too in human history. Whosoever wants to be successful must note that: Success is impossible in any sphere of life without courage and boldness.

If, today, our society is slow in accepting reforms its only cause is that the foundation of our life is based

Courage and Fearlessness

only on defense. We have no courage to go forward. Persons having courage and valor can be counted on the fingers of ones hand.

Those who have no courage or boldness move only to maintain their present status. They do not have any idea of progress or advancement. Even if they opportunities in their life they are unable to take any advantage from them. On the contrary, when courageous people find any possibility of betterment and change they take its full advantage even by suffering hardships.

We should know that every progress and every change demands hard work and patience. Pain is always present at every corner of life. When a baby wants to come to this world from its mother's womb it has to struggle through a narrow passage.

Bold people, when they reach any crossroad in their life, they bear every hardship with a smiling face.

It has been observed that many people are not happy with their present position but since they have no courage they are unable to bear hardships and difficulties for improving their condition. Thus they remain where they are and continue lamenting throughout their lives.

Self Sacrifice

The importance of high and holy aims is much more than physical comfort and material possessions in the eyes of the wise and intelligent people. Only he can get success in such aims that does not care for his life and other material things.

If one aims to attain holy goals for the benefit of his body or life or for material progress it would be a kind of madness, because holy aims demand sacrifice and sacrifice means being unmindful of life, and it is lunacy to sacrifice ones life for material things.

However if one has so much affection and love for a religious aim that it is dearer to him than his life and body and material gains then, in that case, sacrifice, that is the losing of life and money and family and material status will be considered a sign of success.

Those who view life from material angle and desire everything only for material benefit are unable to show the correct reason of the sacrifices offered by the prophets, pious leaders, Imams, great people, selfless diplomats and person having religious and spiritual aims.

It is possible that the materialists may look at those sacrifices as a legend, myth or fiction, and even brand those great persons as lunatics. But one who gives preference to his aim over his life throws himself in dangers with a smiling face and a heart full of lofty sentiments.

Prophet Isa (a.s.) suffered so many difficulties and tolerated the taunts of the Jews only for a Holy aim, which was dearer to him than his life.

Hazrat Ali (a.s.) slept on the bed of the Holy Prophet (s.a.w.a.) on the night of migration (Hijrat). It was the same kind of sacrifice.

If the leader of the martyrs, Imam Husain (a.s.) colored the soil of Kerbala with his blood and that of his near and dear companions, it too was the result of the said love for a holy aim. In his eyes a respectful and honorable death was better than a life of dishonor.

His philosophy was: A red death is better than a black life.

In the battle of Naharawan, a youth, on his own, took a copy of the holy Quran from the Commander of the Faithful (a.s) and went to the battlefield only to be cut into pieces by the enemy, it was also because of his love for his aim. He wanted that truth should overcome falsehood.

Self Sacrifice

If Columbus discovered America, it was his act of sacrifice. He was an expert seaman and had made several voyages of the Atlantic since the age of fourteen.

Columbus and started his voyage on 3rd October 1492 with a convoy of three ships. After tolerating many hardships, dangerous storms, ailments and harsh words of his companions, he reached the shore of America at last.

If, on 6th April 1909, Robert Edwin Perry reached the North Pole it was also his sacrifice. This American seaman, along with his five companions, had reached there only after suffering several difficulties. Perry himself was the captain. After reaching there he made many calculations to fix the exact position of the North Pole. Thereafter he rested for 36 hours continuously. The fingers of his feet had, due to the freezing cold, become useless. His companion, Methinan, amputated those four fingers while Perry was asleep. On the return voyage all the five fingers of his other feet too became useless.

Difficulties and Calamities

In the roaring sea of life there are storms as well as mountain high waves. The high-rise waves of incidents and accidents try to block the paths of great people. Success comes only those who pave their way by tearing the oceans of difficulties riding on the ship of wisdom and planning, and plough through the seas of hardships with the help of the oars of knowledge and intelligence. All this requires firmness as described before. The remarkable point is that the existence of difficulties is one of the causes of success. Some people do not realize this easily, but if they think over it they would realize that just as the heat of fire strengthens steel, difficulties and hardships make the imagination and thinking of man more sharp and teach him the lesson of living.

Strong and powerful people are those who were brought up amidst difficulties and hardships because they alone knew how to cope up with adversities, but those who are nourished in comfort and ease are like delicate and tender flowers, which fall down even by a cold whiff of breeze.

The Master of the Pious, Ali (a.s), who was exemplarily strong physically, extraordinarily high spiritually and unparalleled in steadfast when in difficulties, in his letter to his governor in Basra, Usman bin Hamid, after describing a little about his own simple food, in a part of that communication, writes: I understand, some of you will say that when Ali bin Abu Talib takes so little food, he must have become extremely weak physically and too feeble to stand before the enemy. But, remember that the wood of a forest tree is hard, whereas, the skin of fresh and green tree is thin and delicate and that the forest tinder flares up sooner and keeps on burning longer.

The trees growing on riverbanks live at ease and are not habituated to storms. But the jungle trees are nourished in tough weather. They grow up in hardships and are fed by the scorching sun, hot winds and scant water.

The communities living in hills and vales are stronger than those who pass their lives in cities and towns. People living in mountains, though deprived of many comforts of life, are able to bear and tolerate more heat and cold as compared to the city-dwellers.

When calamity befalls one he uses his intelligence to find out ways of removing it. Really speaking hardships raise the capability of finding solutions of problems and treatments of ailments. Thus difficulties provide steps to climb the ladder to success.

Difficulties and Calamities

Those who have earned name and fame in the field of science and industry have tolerated difficulties almost throughout their lives.

Therefore, Napoleon used to say, "Hardships sharpen man's intelligence, which result in a better gain. Goethe says, "The storms of incidents strengthen the soul and morale of man."

Parents who always want to save their children from every kind of hardship make them tender. They are suffering from a serious misunderstanding. Such tender children tremble like thin leaves in times of stormy weather and fear every breeze. The burdens of life break them down pitiably.

But those who have suffered hazards and tough times keep standing like mountains. Stormy winds cannot harm them at all. Similarly floods always digs up soft ground but hard soil remains intact amidst floods.

The deluge of difficulties proves ineffective in front of tough and sturdy men. Feeble persons cannot stand straight even on their own legs.

The calamities of life provide man with a treasure of experiences and become a ladder to climb up to success and progress. Man gains experience only through hardships. In the light of those experiences he does only those deeds continuously that give him advantage. He marches forward crushing the mountains of hardships under his feet. No calamity can ever come in the path of his advancement. When the arrows of distress hit his chest he tolerates the pain with a smiling face.

Nietzsche says: I love you so much; I wish you should see pains and sorrows. I show no mercy to you in this matter because I really love you. You already know, why? It is so because I wish that your hidden abilities should blossom and that you should combat hard times with an armed soul.

In the words of Nasir Khusro: Man never becomes perfect until he sees sorrow and difficulties. Can a flower spread fragrance without suffering the onslaught of winds and rains?

It would not be wrong to say that the success our children is hidden in hardships. If we say that steel becomes harder after entering fire, a knife becomes sharper only after being grinded on hard rock, it is the same truth.

A brave Persian named Nadir Shah was a great warrior. His wisdom, acquaintance with his job and his zeal are all recorded in books of history. He had

Difficulties and Calamities

undertaken his task in the most difficult condition. In these days a few Afghans had subdued the ancient Persians. Ottoman Turks had occupied the north-western part of Iran, England and Holland were holding southern Iran and the Persian Gulf was in their hands and they intended to make south Iran a second India.

Nadir Shah was finding it difficult to manage law and order due to the luxurious life of his predecessors. But then a brave man like Nadir Shah arose, who was brought up in scorching heat and on burning sandy lands and which had made him accustomed to face and combat all kinds of hazards and wars. The difficulties of life and the disgraceful condition of Iran had turned his body and soul as strong as the collective bodies of the Persian masses.

Employing his enraged soul and his rock-like determination, he cleared Iran of the enemies and thus his name began to be listed as the world's most outstanding warriors.

Torments and tribulations polish man's personality, because he uses his mental faculties for removing difficulties. Hence wise people say that games and sports raise the mental abilities of a child because in the course of games and sports he faces some sort of difficulties and uses his intelligence to remove them.

From this viewpoint, unless there are storms of difficulties many capabilities cannot grow. Hardships and calamities are like a strict teacher whose class scores the best marks.

Objection Raised by Materialists

They say if God is Merciful then why has He engulfed man in calamities? What is the philosophy behind all these problems?

How are these hardships in conformity with God's justice and Mercy as theists claim?

But these worshippers of the material world have ignored one point and it is that these difficulties and hardships too have an aspect of psychological advantage. It is a fact that man does not realize the importance of ease and health until he comes across calamities. Moreover, it is essential to stem the hardships because man requires a warning signal in his life that he may defend himself. If there were no difficulties, man would become selfish and proud. From this angle, these troubles wash off the rust deposited on hearts and fill them with compassion and mercy.

We must never hope that we can achieve a great goal without facing difficulties. Many scientists have succeeded only because of hardships and dearth of means. For example:

Ferguson manufactured a wooden clock with the help of a little knife.

Newton analyzed light with the help of a binocular and a piece of paper and postulated the theory of seven colors.

When the laboratory of the physicist, Weston was visited, only a few bottles, some pieces of papers, a watch and a thermometer were found therein.

Ferguson used to walk out of the town during nights, lie on the open ground under the sky, gazing at the stars measuring the distance between them with the help of a rosary.

A famous space scientist Wittonhouse used to calculate details about solar and lunar eclipses with the help of a small farming implement.

Hardships adorn man with the virtues of manliness. All the high positions, be they material or spiritual, are the fruits of hardships. It is incumbent upon them to overcome the difficulties.

Saib Tabrizi says: Until polished, defects remain in a mirror. One who stubs his toes becomes an expert in his field.

This is really true. The possibility of victory is less for those who have enjoyed ease from the beginning of their lives and are afraid of difficulties. But the youth who has seen both hardship and comfort is more likely to lead his life successfully, because he has already learnt to face calamities right from his childhood.

Accepting the Reality

We must accept the reality or truth, as it does not matter whether it is in our interest or against us. We must never imagine the reality to be always in our favor.

Everyone should wear a spectacle, which can show him the facts honestly, and he too should view them honestly, without any prejudice.

Those who want to spread corruption in society always create rumors to satisfy their mean souls. So as a result of continuously deceiving their hearts they tend to believe their own lies making their minds blind.

On 6th August 1945, the first atom bomb was dropped on the Japanese city of Hiroshima, which has become the world's unforgettable city due to this unfortunate event. The bomb afflicted 1,50,000. Its population, which was 3,44,000 in 1940, was reduced to only 286 in 1953. Three days later a bomb fell on another Japanese city of Nagasaki. The Japanese surrendered a week later. The whole world condemned the beastly act of America, which had mercilessly massacred thousands of innocent men, women and children. This barbarous deed is unprecedented in world history. It was president Truman who had ordered this bombing, whose heart began to trouble his mind thereafter. All the peace lovers of the world condemned Truman whose status was reduced to dust. The world called him a killer instead of a diplomat.

Now, let us see, how Truman had viewed this event and how he was deceiving his soul, distorting the truth and trying to present poison as nectar. He says, "I had issued this order to save millions of American soldiers. If the bombs had not been deployed the U.S. army would have had to attack the shores of Japan, which was very secure with military arrangements. Thus it would have been a furious battle in which Japanese too would have suffered much.

These are the words of an expresident of America, but even a layman can understand that Truman was deceiving himself through false arguments. He did not want to see the reality. Moreover, he has been thinking that his prestige has remained intact and also his popularity, but very soon he tested the fruits of his folly. Freedom lovers of the world threw him out of the field of politics and public life and this stain remained on him forever.

Businessmen, diplomats and other people can succeed in their fields only when they see their conditions truthfully and without any bias. It is necessary for a good trader to listen to the criticism made by the customer about his merchandise or about the way he conducts business with a cool mind and full attention and thereafter remove objectionable things. Similarly it is necessary for a diplomat to consider people's objections properly. Without proper understanding he should not brand the people's movements as self-motivated struggles. He should not try to suppress people by alleging that they are anarchists or lawless. Politicians should always remember that only by loving the truth and appreciating it can a nation be made stable, and their politics secure. Truthfulness is the first condition.

The student who loves progress tolerates the teacher's scolding happily. When he gets fewer marks he never alleges that the teacher was partial. Rather he pays attention and examines his own self and his method of study. Possibly the truth was that he himself had made mistakes and faults. Such understanding of truth will serve him as a ladder to future success.

The Holy Prophet (s.a.w.a.) used to assess the enemies and their power before waging a war against the polytheists and idol-worshippers. He used to gather relevant information before starting a campaign. The facts were sometimes unpleasant too but he never considered the strength of the enemy insignificant and worth ignoring. He never deceived himself or the Muslims through wishful thinking, saying, for instance, that we will finish the enemy with a single assault or will push them into the sea instantly.

In the battle of Badr, Muslim spies captured a soldier of the polytheist Quresh on the well of Badr and brought him to the Holy Prophet (s.a.w.a.). They had not, till then, known the number of the enemy forces.

The Holy Prophet (s) asked him, "How many camels are being slaughtered by the Quresh daily?"

The captured man replied, "Some times nine sometimes ten." The Holy Prophet said, "The enemy's strength is between nine hundred and one thousand men."

The 6-day war between the Arabs and the Israel in June 1967 ended in the defeat of the Arabs. It is painful to state that very few have confessed this bitter truth only because it is bitter. The fact is that the cause of the defeat was that the heads of the Arab states and their internal and external supporters, instead of making a correct and truthful assessment continued to sing and broadcast war songs. Had they done so they would have never faced such a humiliating defeat unparalleled in human history.

Indeed, doubt is a ladder to surety and trust. So long as a man does not develop doubt about anything he does not care to make inquires and act seriously.

Similarly objection and criticism also are ladders leading to perfection. Successful is one who listens to people's criticism carefully. He takes into account every criticism, which has been made selflessly with an intention of improvement. The truth is that true reflection of man and his defects are seen in the mirror of public criticism.

Jamshed made the Jame Jahan Numa (world reflector cup) only because he was not aware of the truth that the world itself is a Jaam (cup) exhibiting itself.

We should remember that Imam Ja'far (a.s.) has said, "Dearest to me among my brothers is the one who presents to me my shortcomings and thus makes me aware of my defects."

In the eyes of our great leaders the best gift is to show the defects of people to them in the nicest possible manner.

In today's free world, criticism is the foundation of life.

The European world invites experts from other countries and entrusts governmental and other departments to them so that they may examine them and offer criticism.

One who feels bad hearing his criticism and who does not like to see the reality as it is and who dislikes to know people's opinion about him, should be told: Break thyself, as it is wrong to break the mirror, which reflects real face.

Flexibility

There is a distinct difference between being flexible and being a weathercock. A flatterer and weathercock type man has no aim in life. He does not follow any true principle. He puts on different masks on his face and appears before others on the stage of life. He destroys all principles for his personal benefits and to satisfy his passions.

But a flexible person behaves mildly unless there is a danger to his principles or aims. He makes agreements even with his enemies when essential. He lets go many of his personal advantages in order to safeguard his principles and if need be, gives preference to the wishes of others ignoring his own liking.

The changing circumstances of the world are mostly like the storms, which uproot many. A windstorm starts and attacks trees. Green trees show some flexibility and allow the storm to pass overhead and soon thereafter become upright after bowing for a while. But dry and hard trees try to remain standing in the face of stormy winds. The hardness and stiffness does not allow them to be flexible and consequently they are uprooted.

The head of a state who is in charge of all affairs, the managing director of an organization who has to deal with hundreds of people, a trader or businessman who faces all kinds of consumers and buyers are such people that if they sacrifice their principles for gaining passing and temporary benefits, they are weathercocks.

But the same people, if they show a little flexibility, become somewhat soft and give some positive response to the demands of relevant people, and win over their hearts by suffering a little material loss then, we can consider them as people having a desirable flexibility.

In this connection, the Holy Prophet (s.a.w.a.) says, "In the face of the storms of events the position of a believer is like a flexible plant. When a stormy wind hits, it shows softness and does not remain stiffly erect. But an unbeliever is like a hard dry tree, which does not bend and consequently gets uprooted."

If these people are harsh in ordinary matters in dealing with different types of people it can harm their reputation. Such harshness creates hatred in the hearts of the masses and, therefore, such people cannot attain high status nor can they perform commendable deeds. Only one with some flexibility in temper can become popular in society.

Flexibility

If you see the Treaty of Hudaibiyah you will be surprised to observe the flexibility shown by the Holy Prophet (s.a.w.a.). The treaty he signed in the 8th year of the Hijri Era with the idolaters of Quresh was even criticized by some ignorant and unwise persons, but with the passage of time it was proved that flexibility was necessary for future success.

The biggest hurdle in the advance of Islam was the idolaters of Quresh. They had, through their continuous attacks taken away the freedom of the Holy Prophet (s.a.w.a). Had there not been this hindrance, the Holy Prophet's call was so effective and impressive that, by dispatching a few preachers and by propagating and spreading the message of the holy Quran, he could have brought the entire Arab Peninsula under the banner of Monotheism. However the idolworshippers had deprived the Holy Prophet of this chance by direct and indirect attacks on him.

The high aim and noble intention of the Holy Prophet was to get secure freedom for propagating Islam. With this aim in view he signed the peace treaty with the Quresh and showed a high and uncommon measure of flexibility.

In order to explain our point we mention hereunder some points:

The Holy Prophet (s.a.w.a.) had entrusted the writing of the treaty to Ali (a.s.) who wrote on the first page: "Bismillahirrehmaanirraheem" (In the Name of Allah, Most Gracious, Most Merciful), but at once the delegate of the Quresh said, "We do not know the words Rahman and Rahim. According to Arabian customs, you should write 'Bismika Allahumma. The Holy Prophet (s.a.w.a) accepted this proposition. Then Ali wrote, "This is an agreement, which has been entered into, by God's Messenger Muhammad with the representative of the Quresh." Immediately the Quresh said, "We do not recognize Muhammad as the messenger of God. Had we recognized him as the prophet of God, we would not have fought him." The Holy Prophet (s.a.w.a.) asked Ali to erase the words "Messenger of God".

One of the conditions of this agreement was that if any polytheist flees Mecca and reaches the Islamic capital of Medina, it would be the responsibility of the Islamic state to return that man to the authorities of Quresh. But if any Muslim runs away from Medina and takes shelter in Mecca the Quresh will not be responsible for returning him to the Muslims.

The Holy Prophet (s.a.w.a.) accepted this condition too so that he and his followers may get some relief from the Quresh, and a path may be opened for propagation of Islam. The advantages he obtained in connection with the propagation of Islam were more important than the allowances he gave to Quresh.

One of the defects of our way of working is that when we calculate our profit and loss, we forget to maintain a balance. If we cut off relations with some people, we do so forever continuously and never think that the relations can be restored under some special conditions. In other words we consider flexibility as a sign of defeat and disgrace. But both wisdom and Shariat say that it is a principle of success to show flexibility to an extent, which does not harm our original aim.

The Correct Way

One of the great economists says, "Financial institutions and factories manufacturing various items decline due to their tendency of maintaining their original position."

Intelligent people believe that to remain in the same condition is a kind of downfall. But is this law only for factories? Or is it a common law applicable to all categories of every kind and every field?

In this respect Ali (a.s.) says, "If a man passes two continuous days in such a way that from the material and spiritual view-point the latter day is just like the former one, then that person has suffered a great loss in his life."

Man's greatest capital is the life span gifted to him. This precious capital is being spent gradually. If its return is not of the same value then it means that we have lost our capital and have not been able to make any profit by it.

As a principle doing new things is a part of human nature. Man becomes bored doing the same work continuously for a long time. Even the most delectable things lose their taste if they are consumed daily.

Shopkeepers and departmental stores owners, in order to avoid monotony, rearrange their materials every now and then even if the profit from both the settings is same.

Newspapers having large circulations, in order to avoid similarity, change printing or color every day or every week, so that it may not appear awkward.

Similarly the decorations of dining halls in big restaurants are changed often so that they appear attractive and people may not be bored.

But is every kind of change and novelty a sign of progress? Is it so even if good thing turns into bad ones? Never!

While the great economists consider changelessness a kind of decline they also consider it suicidal to change a good thing into a bad one. From this viewpoint, every change should be proper and it should be better than earlier. When we make an improvement we should not concentrate only upon its outer change, but we must also pay attention to the original aim and make changes accordingly.

The main defect of our eastern factories is that when once the masses like their products they never think

The Correct Way

of making any changes and if they ever do so they do not do it in a nice way.

The Holy Prophet always liked regularity, discipline and aptness in every work.

When a military officer Saad bin Maaz died and his coffin was lowered in the grave, the Holy Prophet (s.a.w.a.) observed that people are dropping dust in it in an inappropriate manner, which made him sorrowful. He sat down near the grave, leveled the earth of the grave with his own hands and then said to his companions, "I know that this grave will soon become old. But God likes a slave who performs his work nicely and perfectly."

The Holy Prophet (s.a.w.a.) knew that this mismanagement and irregularity could enter every walk of life. He did not like that even a minor and ordinary work should be done haphazardly even if it was not to last long.

Any young man or woman that desires appreciation of his deeds and one who aims for permanent success should perform today's work in a way better than yesterday.

Unexpected Success

The system of the universe is based on the law of cause and effect. Even the minutest happening is not an exception to this universal law.

The roaring of the ocean, the falling of the leaves, snowfall, rain, the difference in palm lines, variance in the faces, rise and fall of nations, social good and evil; in short each and everything is bound by this law of cause and effect. Sometimes the reason is apparent and sometimes it is hidden from us. Therefore there is no place for a 'chance'. No philosophy of the world can prove the existence of 'chance'. To rely on chance is, in fact, to repose trust in an imaginary thing, which is far from reality. Unwise and ignorant people think that good or bad luck is connected with this unbecoming imagination.

Luck, accident, chance and fortune etc. are, really speaking, superstitions. Only people who are unaware of the underlying causes of various happenings mention them. They tend to believe in such things just to please their condemning conscience by trusting such unreal causes.

If at all, we have to trust in 'chance' then we should say that only endeavor, work, struggle and activeness provide the basis of 'chance' and 'good luck'. This invisible cause lies behind activeness and hard work.

Trust in luck is only an instrument for remaining idle and for misleading the mind. It is a tranquilizer for soothing the heart of idle and inactive persons. In other words, reliance on luck is a cover to conceal the conscience of sinners and wrongdoers.

If a player loses a game and the medal is awarded to someone else, he comes out of the playground with a dark face and a forehead wet with perspiration and, in order to retrieve his loss tells his friends something like, "The luck of my rival was better. Hence he won. This time my fortune was not favorable and therefore I lost." What is pitiable is that, for avoiding a future defeat, he does not find out the real causes of his failure. Rather he resorts to imaginary causes, which have no basis from the viewpoint of knowledge, intelligence and philosophy or logic. He wants that he should not be held responsible for the defeat.

The fact is that there is an incorrect tradition in our society according to which they make luck or fortune the basis of life with regard to family affairs, educational matters and trade etc. Parents, teachers and traders create such conditions whereby people automatically attribute success and defeat to be the effect of chance and luck. The harmful effects of this wrong tradition fill the minds of people during childhood, youth as well as in old age.

A little verse in Quran, which is small in words but very great in meaning, has refuted all such imaginary things. It declares: "Man gets only that for which he strives."

Like lottery, gambling and such other things resorting to luck harms our society grievously by making our youths believe in such imaginary things and thus deprive them of an enthusiasm for work and struggle. Thereafter, instead of utilizing their mental and physical powers, they begin to rely on imaginary things, like luck, for attaining success, position and wealth etc. in life.

Only those ladies and gentlemen are successful in whose dictionaries there are no words like chance, star, palmistry etc. because they are like iron chains binding the hands and feet of people.

Youths who wants to attain progress and perfection and utilize their capabilities should know that the real reason and cause of the success of any student, inventor, military officer or diplomat is that he has realized the reality of life and has adopted the true tools of success the list of which is headed by work, endeavor, steadfastness and discipline. He must understand that no star, magic or chance can ever be the cause of any success or victory.

One of my friends has recently returned from Germany. Regarding the success of the German people he says, "Within a very short time, this community has, sparing very few things as memorials, destroyed every sign showing the devastation caused by the World War in such a way that now, it seems, no loss was inflicted on them by the enemy bombs a few years ago."

The lively soul and strong mind of this community proved to be the cause of its success. They never relied on chance and luck. They relied only on their mental and physical abilities. They knew very well that if there is anything like luck it is hidden behind the mental and physical capabilities.

Luck, Stars and Predictions etc.

A wise man has said, "Only a nation which has not realized facts takes shelter behind futile and imaginary things."

A loss-making businessman makes himself happy by dreaming success. A defeated nation hopes for victory by looking at palm lines and lucky draws. Sick womenfolk, instead of going to a physician, fall in the trap of magicians and fortune-tellers.

Superstitious and unwise ignorant parents fill the minds of their children with futile and imaginary things. They think that the Wednesday following marriage and the rituals performed on the fourteenth day after the Navroz festival are steps to success. On the thirteenth day after Navroz they take their children to a forest and ask them to tie knots on long grass leaves so that their ambitions may be fulfilled and the luck which has become angry at them may return to their lives.

The parents tell their children that if they sit on a tablecloth full of seven kinds of food while holding a red colored purse in hands would surely become wealthy.

Our beloved Prophet (s.a.w.a.) always opposed such beliefs in all the fields of life and at every stage.

One day, his foster mother sent him for a walk in the forest with her own sons and hung a small Omani green stone in his neck so as to protect him from calamities. The Holy Prophet (s.a.w.a.) removed it and said, Mother, what a superstition is this. My protector is someone else (Allah).

Sometimes, a van driver, instead of taking care of the break tires etc., and instead of replacing old parts with new ones, takes shelter behind superstitious matters. He fixes horseshoe at the back of his vehicle and believes that it would be safe from mishaps.

An armed dacoit gets ten years' rigorous imprisonment. When he enters the prison he blackens the walls with couplets like this:

No astrologer could recognize the star of my luck. O God! What a kind of luck I am born with!

He is so unaware, and his own words show that while suffering the torments of the prison he is not prepared to understand the reality. In order to satisfy his chiding soul he attributes his crimes to stars and luck. He does not understand that he has

misused arms and endangered public peace; that shops and business establishments closed down due to his mischief and that he deserves this punishment.

Instead of the above quoted couplet he should have written these couplets of Nasir Khusro:

Do not blame the blue sky. Drive out the wind of carelessness from your head. If you spoil your luck by your own carelessness, you should not hope for success from the sky. The wood of a leafless tree is being burnt down by people. This indeed is the punishment of not taking care of the tree of life. If the fruits of knowledge and intelligence grow on the tree of your life, such a tree can even bring down the sky.

He alone is successful who marches forward on the path of his aim and refrains from entertaining all kinds of superstitions and baseless things.

The Holy Prophet (s.a.w.a.) strived hard, especially to free the people from the bonds of superstitions. Even if a baseless thought was in his favor he used to tell the people, "Such a belief is baseless."

For example, the Holy Prophet's son Ibrahim expired. There was a solar eclipse that day. Superstitious people went to the Holy Prophet and said, "The calamity, which has befallen you, is so great that the sun too is mourning. This eclipse is due to the death of your dear son."

In response, the Holy Prophet (s.a.w.a.) uttered this historical sentence, "O People! Sun and moon do not mourn anybody's death. Rather, the lunar and solar eclipses are the signs of Allah's power. (Eclipse has a special reason. It should not be attributed to my son's demise)."

Superstitious People of the West

Some Westerners are so superstitious that they are afraid of engaging a room numbered 13 in a hotel.

Therefore the hoteliers do not use the number 13 but make it "12+1" or 14 and completely omit the figure of 13! It is said that in United Nations headquarters the lift reaches floor No. 14 after floor No. 12; that there is no floor No. 13; that in fact floor number 13 is called floor 14!!

These people do not think, or do not want to think at all that if the 13th floor is inauspicious and dangerous, that thing would not change merely by changing its name.

Shaikh Saadi relates a beautiful story in one of his poems: The donkey of a villager died.

He cut off its head and hung it on a grapevine.

When an experienced old man passed by it, he told the gardener of the villager laughingly:

"O dear! Do not think that this donkey will protect the garden from an evil eye?

While alive, it could not prevent the charge of a stick on its head from the hand of a weak man.

So, how can it, after its death, save the garden from an evil eye?"

A same type of man had such deep belief in luck that he used to say, "I have come in this world with a bad fortune. It is so bad that if I been a capmaker people would be born without heads!"

If such superstitions spread in any society, particularly among the youth, it should be considered as one of the causes of that society's decline.

Blaming the Stars!

Some people keep on complaining against stars and some throw the blame of their bad conditions on the outer space. Some writers even blame the sky in their books!!

However the fact is that the sky has been helpful to man since Allah has created it for the benefit of mankind. For example, the sun nourishes the animals through its golden rays. The moon spreads freshness in the atmosphere and provides cool light. So the things, which serve man, should not be called oppressors.

There is no inauspiciousness in the sun, the moon, the stars or the sky because, God has sworn by them in the holy Quran thus showing us their importance.

We must keep in mind that if some authors and intellectuals have ever complained against the sky, they have, thereby, meant the men living under it. Otherwise the sky and the stars revolving therein are never at fault.

Waiting for a Chance

It cannot be denied that sometimes incidents do ease man's difficulties and that everybody experiences such chances in his or her life. History has recorded many of such incidents and chances some of which are as under:

1. Imadud Daulah occupied Isfahan and Faris and threw out the governor of Isfahan. Not before long his army's provisions were exhausted. He was afraid that his men would loot the property of people and infuriate them. Thinking this he looked at the ceiling and saw a snake poking its head out of a hole and then withdrawing it. The snake repeated this action several times. He ordered the demolition of the roof to find out where the hole of the snake leads. When they reached the other end of that snake-hole they found some utensils full of golden coins stored for emergency by a former ruler of the territory. Imadud Daulah ordered they all be taken out. Thus he was saved from a big financial crisis.

2. After defeating Amr Laith, Shah Ismail Samani met with financial crisis. Soldiers were likely to plunder public wealth. So he ordered the soldiers to vacate the city. While marching out the soldiers saw a crow flying over their heads with a necklace in its beak. They followed the bird, which dropped that necklace in a well. At

the command of the king some soldiers went down the well to find therein a box full of precious stones. Slaves of Amr Laith had hidden it at the time of his arrest but could not take it out thereafter.

3. Shaikh Muslihuddin Sadi Shirazi has narrated a story about a shooting contest: A prince had placed a narrow ring at a high place so that sharp shooters may try to pass their arrow though it and earn a big reward. All the expert archers failed.

In the meanwhile a man who did not know even the basics of archery tried and hit the target and got the prize.

But can such stories guide people and can a man ever rely on such chances?

The proportion of success through chance is much less that that achieved by efforts and incidence of success by chance is very less. It also happens that chance gives a fruit bitter than poison. Wise men never sit idle waiting for a chance. They never ignore apparent causes and fall in a superstitious chance. Such chances are less than one in thousands.

Waiting for a Chance

Suppose 10,00,000 people live in a city. An airplane is about to drop two gold coins in the city. Can one leave his business keeping his eye on that plane?

If we do so and if our pocket is empty our stomach too would remain empty!!

Those nations, which do not rely on their own efforts and await favorable global conditions for drawing mercy from them, are sure to be destroyed.

A student who does not study and awaits an unusual happening bestowing him good marks by chance is never likely to succeed.

One of the religious leaders of Islam has said something which is very important in the eyes of the wise people: "A nation that has natural resources on land and in water but does not utilize these great divine blessings and becomes poor, the Almighty Allah would drive it away from His Mercy."

No nation of the world has ever won nor any individual ever succeeded without utilizing the apparent natural causes. They must have taken the trouble to walk towards the goal with a strong faith in Allah's Omnipotence, without waiting for favorable chances.

In the words of a poet:

A great man must have a greater resolution to solve his difficulties.

Freedom depends on the sword. So great people always rely on it.

It is a law of nature that those who get habituated to rest, ease and luxury,

Are sure to be weakened.

May be some people or nations get some success owing to

chance. But success resulting through chance is as baseless as winning a gamble.

In the words of a wise man: "A short cut is most difficult and dangerous. Though long routes do take more time to pass through but man reaches his destination safely and easily." Sometimes man also reaches his destination via short cuts. But if a nation remains idle waiting for a short cut it is doomed.

Advanced societies never wait for chances, but idle and lazy people who do not even want to think always say: "Just see this chance! Man must be so lucky... "

Waiting for a Chance

However, a thing, which has never contributed to the success of the nations, is something called 'coincidence' or 'chance'. If the advanced people have ever got a chance it was the chance to work and to strive.

Those who do not want to perspire and want to scale great heights via the imaginary staircase of 'chance' fall down before they could go any further.

It is said that an apple incidentally fell on Newton and he discovered one of the greatest laws of (the law of gravity). However there is misunderstanding here as people have seen such things several times but never discovered any laws from them.

The truth is that Newton possessed the necessary means for finding out the said law. He thought over it and had studied and any other man of thought and research too could have made such a discovery.

If a scientist analyzed light by observing the foam of soap it was not chance. He had done studied and worked on that subject earlier. Otherwise washer men see such bubbles every day but derive nothing from them and never discover any law.

Incorrect Understanding of Destiny

When we say that luck is imaginary and illusory, it does not mean that Divine religions and the holy Quran has said so. What we mean is that some simple-minded people think that they are captives of luck and that someone else makes and unmakes their destiny.

We may be theists or materialists; we may be of the opinion that some 'intellect' controls the management of the universe thoughtfully and with a planning; or we may say that the universe has come into existence by chance through the coming together of innumerable atoms.

Anyway we cannot deny that ever since a young man has started drinking he has made his future dark for himself and ruined his luck. After some time he would end up in a hospital with a damaged kidney then either his heart would fail or his nerves break.

We are sure that a man who does not know how to control carnivorous animals should not start playing with the tail of a lion or a cheetah. Otherwise he would become a morsel for them within no time.

Surely when a gambler loses he himself is responsible for his bad luck.

Someone has said quite correctly: It is madness, not misfortune to lean out precariously from the terrace and then fall down. Work is the best wing to fly in the sky of knowledge. Art is the best wealth in the world. You should keep trying even if your aim is beyond imagination and you must continue walking even if your path passes through the mouth of a python.

A successful student who had studied day and night has improved his destiny ever since he entered the university.

To summarize, our efforts today construct our future. Worldly affairs are interconnected like the rings of a chain. If an intermediary ring breaks off the whole series or scheme of life is disturbed. Every ring is the cause for another.

Every happening is based on a series of causes and effects. For example, today's events will become the cause for tomorrow's events. Similarly the causes of tomorrow will be the reasons for the happenings of the day after. The story of future is inscribed on the forehead of the present day. Previous events themselves tell us that today's happenings are the

Incorrect Understanding of Destiny

harbingers of tomorrow's events. The relation between the two is unmistakable. If somebody ponders over the management of the Creator he can clearly predict tomorrow's events.

If we read in religious books or in the holy Quran that man lives within the limits of destiny or if it is written in the holy Quran that whatever you do has been inscribed in the Lauhe Mahfuz (Protected Tablet) from the beginning, it does not mean that we are the prisoners of destiny and are bound to act accordingly. Rather what is meant thereby is that the Omniscient God is aware of all the events of the past and the future and knows who will work voluntarily for what and will consequently decide his own good or bad fortune.

Allah is aware of what man will do but man is absolutely free to shape his destiny.

A Wrong Notion About Destiny

Some people deceive themselves and ignore the voice of their intellects. The mind, in the words of Rumi, says:

When you say I will do this or that, my dear! It is the proof of your freedom of action.

Some people think that they are born helpless and that they have no freedom of action at all. In their opinion they are like stones dropped from above that cannot do anything except falling down.

Or they are like a plant, which grows and flourishes in a certain way by which it is bound. They think against the dictates of their intellect and that of the nature. Everyone knows that he is free to do what he likes. He himself shapes his own destiny.

Force of Environment

If, in earlier days, people used to blame destiny for the bad effects of their wrong deeds, people today say that environment is responsible for the adverse effects of their bad deeds. They are deceiving themselves and trying to cover up their own misdeeds.

Let us see what is the 'Force of environment', which is mentioned in some social and philosophical books.

What they mean is that it is in the interest of man to meet the demands of time and to live according to the times.

For example, today, people share the benefits of modern technology. They travel by airplanes; rest under the shades of electricity (air conditioning) and modern techniques are utilized in the educational field etc. Thus man has to walk with the society and has to act like others. We accept the 'force of environment' upto this limit.

However some people take undue benefit and blame the society and the environment for their own wrong ways and if the young generation is being spoilt they say, "The youths are not to blame because the environment is bad." Such people make a mockery of reason and logic. They are themselves responsible for the consequences because were free to act rightly or wrongly.

Under the Shade of Allah's blessings

It is necessary to mention here that though man is free to make or unmake his destiny, it does not mean that he needs no one else and that he can do everything without the help of Allah. Such a theory is neither accepted by the Divine scriptures nor by intelligence and logic. However strong a man may be, he is after all created by Allah——God has created him and he needs innumerable things to live. He uses the energy given by God for fulfilling his needs.

Man is like an electric bulb, which needs to remain connected with the powerhouse for remaining on. But he is free to light up either a mosque or a nightclub.

If man realizes that he is connected with the limitless power of Allah, he will never become lazy. Rather his working power will increase, because he will be aware of the fact that a great source of power is backing him, and that he has not been left alone to suffer the hardships of this world.

Soldiers who remain in the front ranks of the army for fighting the enemy can fight courageously only when they are confident that they are sufficiently backed. Without such assurance they would become nervous.

Giving instruction in a battlefield Ali (a.s.) had advised his son: My Son! Remember that real help comes only from Allah.

Inherited Wealth

A friend of mine used to say about the children of rich people born with a silver spoon in mouth and who get a high position due to their family prestige: Some people are lucky right from the womb and they possess a very good fortune.

He thought that good luck depended on riches and luxuries and that a man born rich remains respectable in the eyes of the people for a period of time and that he need not make any effort.

I do not accept this opinion at all. It is true that a man's progress is made easier by the honorable position of his parents and family wealth. Man can obtain considerable assistance from these things. But it should not be forgotten that if a boy born rich does not get proper guidance he becomes more helpless and degraded than a poor child.

Prestige and wealth of the parents can make their children lucky only when they do not indulge in immorality and vices owing to the inherited wealth. Alas! It seldom happens that God-given blessings are utilized in the right path. Most of the time the consequences are not good.

History testifies that prophets were born and bred in poor homes and that great men used to live in huts before scaling great heights in the social framework.

It is even said that in special circumstances poverty proves to be the cradle of intelligence and History and experience prove this to be true.

The Seal of the poets, Abu Tamam has written *Hamasah* and other nice books. He was born in a poor home, and had to work as a water carrier to maintain himself.

The greatest book of Geography in the Muslim world, *Mojamul Buldan* was written in the seventh century of the Hijri ear. Its author, Yaqoob Hamawi was merely a slave. His

master, Ibrahim Hamawi, used to send him on business tours to different cities and he used to note down the geographical conditions of each place. At last he compiled ten big volumes from his notes. Even today, this book is referred to whenever one wants to know the actual conditions of these cities in that era.

A great intellectual like Amir Kabir was the son of a cook born in a society, which had suffered many atrocities of oppressive rulers. Those experiences were so severe that they turned him into a courageous and a confident man.

Inherited Wealth

Sir Thomas Lawrence was the son of an unemployed father but he had intelligence and other capabilities. He could learn poems by heart at the age of five. At sixteen he was awarded a prize for drawing a picture on the occasion of an annual festival by 'The Association of Artists'.

Napoleon says, "Wealth is a deadly weapon in the hands of a youth by which he kills himself and his relatives."

An Arabic language poet says: "Youth, unemployment and richness destroy a man badly."

We had said earlier that unless these blessings are utilized in a wise way they prove harmful. Correct guidance is necessary in this matter.

Shaikh Sadi says: When Syria witnessed turmoil, all went into corners. Unwise sons of the minister went to the villagers begging and village beggars became the ministers of the king.

There is a Persian proverb: Poverty is the mother of inventions.

There was a time when Japanese markets were full of European goods till they halted the imports of foreign goods and the Japanese prime minister announced, "Until shoes are not manufactured in Japan all Japanese people should walk barefoot." Then they started to progress in every field and consequently became self-reliant and produced all kinds of goods from their raw material.

The lineage of Shakespeare is not known exactly but all say that he was the son of a butcher and himself cleaned wool in his childhood. It is also said that he worked as a school peon. Thereafter be became a writer. But this very intelligent man possessed the essence of many experiences. He had worked in almost all the fields, which increased his knowledge, study and wisdom. He began to compose poetry and his poetic compositions are considered masterpieces of the literary world even today.

From a Tailoring Shop to the Presidential Chair

President Andrew Jackson was well known for his wisdom and knowledge. He gave a long speech in Washington and described various stages of his life and said that at first he was a tailor and then rose to presidency passing though many stages. When people looked astonished he told them, "People look at me with contempt as I was a tailor in the beginning. But I never felt ashamed to work as a tailor. When I was tailor I was well known as an honest and expert artisan. I used to give tailored clothes to my clients in time and all were pleased with my work."

We have also seen the children of great people who fell into bad times due to lack of proper guidance. But, contrary to it, we have also seen youths who have improved their conditions themselves and have scaled the ladder of progress.

History proves that whether in the field of education and morality or crafts and politics, only those have proved to be great who got some position due to their own learning, hard work and ability. No other factor has been responsible for their progress and success.

www.ingramcontent.com/pod-product-compliance
Lightning Source LLC
Chambersburg PA
CBHW021442070526
44577CB00002B/253